The Golden Layered Onion

The Bittersweet Pain of Post-Traumatic Stress Disorder

The Journal of a Child Sex Slave, from a Child's Point of View

by Ciddd

D1616855

The Golden Layered Onion:
the Bittersweet Pain of Post-Traumatic Stress Disorder
The Journal of a Child Sex Slave, from a Child's Point of View

Love, Ciddd

Eye to eye

The Golden Pearl Army has sent me here, and I am a nurse angel to doctor up as many wounds as possible and to give relief, even to those who have done things wrong, and those who have done things right. God has mercy; unfortunately, there are consequences. We reap what we sow. It's that easy.

"You"

Your soul feels empty
Your heart is ripping
Your knees are shaking
You know it's here.
The dark black tunnel
The long scary road ahead.
Your vision has changed
You can't sea anything
But you know what's there.
Where do you run?
Who can you trust?
In the mist of darkness,
"You" are the only one.
- The Slayereth

Girl
When the little girl comes out to play
She has to be under control of the devil.
When she's running with the devil
She has no life. You call it life.
You call it safety. You call it
Well behaved.

For the darkness knows no light until it shines bright and
The light of the tunnel is there.
To all my fellow man, the light is inside deep like the deepest of the sea
Where big beautiful octopuses roam
Working for the golden light from above.
There is hope and relief ahead, my fellow man,
It is right here now.
Watch its moves.
It's there, my fellow man,
Look and you shall find it.
Thank you for reading this book.
I can sea you reading it and having hope.
Not all feel this much pain and suffering.
Some have spaces with light in them.
I can't stop helping you.
 - Love, Cid

Please note: names have been changed to protect the innocent and the guilty.

Sorry to everybody that they have to read horrific realities, but sometimes we need shock treatment.

So, please read at your own risk. There is sexual content in the book. This book is rated "R" – parental discretion is advised.

The truth shall set us free. This story is my life as a child sex slave and my post-traumatic stress disorder (PTSD) gift and duty to the children of the entire planet. Please try to read the whole thing. As I write this book and then sea the Golden onion layers unfold. As the onion layers unfold to a long journey through the unknown of a brain who survived a monster, friend, family member, who tricked everyone into denial. How hard it is to wrap this kinda life hidden behind the light. This journey through the sad realization that we have a huge responsibility to help those who are sick, who have the DNA of child sex offenders, and those who have the desire for children that can refrain from their desires. We have to be able to be truthful so that we can help the human race.

The Golden Layered Onion:
The Bittersweet Pain of Post-Traumatic Stress Disorder –
The Journal of a Child Sex Slave

Introduction

In this book, I share my experiences and my opinions from what I have learned from being trapped with a child molester for seven years as a child sex slave. Introduction of awareness of children's scary monsters that live on our planet, which we know as pedophiles; however, not all pedophiles are child molesters. Not all can stop themselves so it's our duty to stop them. There are pedophiles who have learned to live and abstain from their sexual urges, and my hat goes off to them. It took many years and many people to put down Larry Lee Dailey, the child molester who got me, but he is now sentenced to over forty years with no chance of parole. His victims, however, suffer.

I am writing this book to help my fellow human of the universe to strengthen their genes and their DNA lines for the future to come, for each and every living being on this planet. The answer is YES, I do have Post-Traumatic Stress Disorder (PTSD), that's what the earthlings call it. It's about awareness.

As a child, I got to live in Hawaii with the hippies in 1972, and nudist colonies in some parts of the ghetto of Hawaii and parts of the rain forest of Hawaii. (Thank God for all of the music that got me through my day-to-day life and I want to thank all of the older rock and roll stars that were there for me, dead and alive ones, I am thanking them all. By the age of two, I had already sean Led Zeppelin in concert.) Thank God for the Hawaiian culture and surf culture, too. Thank God for the water because without the water, I'd be dead right now. Without the water, I wouldn't be alive.

When I was 13 and I was just set free, it was like I got out of a dark cave; not a pretty one, though. I love caves, but this cave, you need tools to survive and to get through it. It's almost as if you would be imagining yourself packing your lunch and in your lunch, you are putting everything in that you like and that is going to satisfy your taste buds and fill your belly, and nourish your body. Those are all tools that you pack for your body's nourishment. That's the same thing that people have to do with PTSD when they go through dark tunnels and come out. They need to repack their tools to get ready in case they go through another dark cave. I am trying to give the world these tools so that they have an awareness to prepare themselves with armor, the Golden Pearl armor.

At 13, I started school for the first time without Larry at home. I got ready to go into 7th grade, and I had home economics. For the first time, at school, I got to be free. It was like when you wind a rubber band up and then all of a sudden they cut it, you spin out. Once it is spun out, you have a lovely rubber band, (but you can't guarantee that the rubber band will be usable; sometimes it might crack or be stretched so far that it can't go back, and it won't be usable for your hair). In Home Economics, I got to make a sewing project, and I picked a purple octopus. I am still in love with that octopus today. The reason that I talk about this as such a significant thing is because I had no conscious brain power left in the cognitive area of my brain due to all the stress and strain that Larry put upon my brain. I had to develop new pockets in my brain because Larry put such a strain that I developed extra brains. But when Larry was gone, the strain was set free and I could consciously remember the purple octopus and the fact that I could sew. The feeling that I got to be free from Larry – someone did come to the door and take me away from it. (My father.) I didn't realize how talented I was (when I made the purple octopus). I still sea billboards, with octopuses on them.

Father God is my savior,
He came to me in the night
And held me tight, and
Set me free.
Ciddd

What good did come out of me to survive pedophilia and rape?
Is it to be a warrior for all my other fellow families around the
universe who are seaking help from pedophilia? They say that there
is always something good from bad, but I promise, we can have
the good; we don't have to have the bad. We do not. Not when
it comes to little people who cannot defend themselves. Not to
change the subject, but I want my mom and my father to know
that it may hurt them to read this book and to know that each one
of them has brought something special to my life, but the truth
will set you free. I believe in freedom. Freedom of choice and birth

rights to protect all humans from sexual abuse, otherwise we will have a world of walking zombies, and we will self-destruct.

It's like I can sea myself being shot through this dark tunnel, cave place and I'm spit out back and forth to the Golden Pearl Army. I am not a man, nor a woman. Right now, as I live on this planet, I am in a very big dark cave, trying to save as many little children as possible. As I write this book, I am in the biggest tunnel I ever could imagine being in. I am grateful to have everyone that reads my book. It's like pouring the vanilla in your cake mix. Oh how sweet!

Also, I may offend some readers who disagree with what I believe, and I am not here to judge anybody, although, if God didn't want us to be aware, he wouldn't have sent me here. And he wouldn't have given us a nervous system so we can be feeling our surroundings. Similar to feeling like crying when we are sad, we have feelings for a reason. We are conscious beings, and the more you become aware of your own gifts, the faster you get to know them, the better.

One of my gifts is that the dead come through me. Lately, it has been males. I have had a couple of females, but mainly males. What I mean by they come through me is that I get messages from the individual. All of a sudden, I may be sitting there watching TV or something, and then I get a moment when I am stopped in time. That is when I get a clear message of the person and what they are telling me. That's all I can say. I feel it is a gift because when I do it, I get gigantic validations and proof that God is giving me work and wanting me to help people that have not been able to settle their way down to feel like they are safe and calm again. Similar to when you know that a bad guy is coming in, and your nervous system cannot relax. That's the kind of validations that I get when the dead come through me.

I am sorry if this book is sad and scary, and if I offend any religious people, but it's time to take the blinders off. It's time to take the rug and clean and hang it outside and let it get some fresh air. So you can sea what's under the rug and clean it.

I was asking the universe, "Are you pleased with me, Father?" when the Lady in Lavender came down with gold bells from the sky, with gold trim; long brown hair with gold ribbons, and gold trimming along her dress and bells in her hands that she could clap together. This is not a joke, this really happened to me. The lavender represented healing and the gold was grateful and bright. That's when I got the vision of the Lady in Lavender. Ever since that I had such an awakening experience; but I have had many more than that. This book is based on a child's point of view of being sexually abused.

A four and a half year old to the age of twelve and a half year old. A sex doll for a manipulative, controlling child molesting monster from his age of twenty years old to twenty eight years old.

The Golden Layered Onion:
The Bittersweet Pain of Post-Traumatic Stress Disorder
The Journal of a Child Sex Slave
July 24, 2014

Scenario

When you live with a child molester, they live in their world, only they control and dictate your every move in your world. Similar to a dream that you can't get out of, and you keep hoping you will wake up. Sweat and tears and anxiety, and sweaty palms, twitching nerves, feeling wretched like a heavy black cloud is pressing on your chest and you are getting just enough to get to the next step, in order for their sexual needs to be met hour to hour. When you (family member, parent, loved one, friend of a child) are alone or with another person, they will work hard at getting your attention away from your own child. They will be very smart, yet dumb at the same time. The more that you are aware of them, the more you will sea that they cannot control their behavior and their world to a point.

There are children around your city who need you desperately to notice what is happening. Every child, meaning babies as well, all human life from birth to any age, who is being molested right at this moment, while we are out dining or working, please watch for these signs. Male or female will work around their prey; they will give them personal attention. They will push to be alone with the child whether it is taking them home in a time of need, or a baseball coach getting on a baseball player whose parents are too strict, and worried about their kid winning, and the coach can pick up on these circumstances so that the coach can scare the child. He can either try to comfort them in times of sorrow, depending on how the pedophile at the moment assesses in his brain his surroundings, or he can control with threats to tell your parents bad things about the game. Sometimes this can go on for a long time before you notice, and then the pedophile has gotten to the child, and then it's too late. Boom. They've got the venom, and you've been bitten.

These species we call pedophiles, child lovers or child molesters, they are very real. Some are very vicious in ways that seem nice and good. It is a hellish day waiting to come your way to your new born baby. I know that this sounds very wretched, and down and negative, and I'm sorry, but the raw truth is that some of these people can be vicious in that they are born with a disease that there is no cure for yet. I know that we love some of them, and we care about some of them, but it is time to stand up and protect our human race. We also have to help the humans learn to be aware of them. Also, they deserve protection as well. They need help. They didn't ask, "God, can I come to earth to be a monster?" There are people born with the DNA of pedophilia. There are some humans that are more open about their love for little people and come out of the closet, so to speak, to help others and themselves. That is the most courageous human effort to protect others that I have ever seen in the history of human beings. Some hide it under marriage and still find a way to the child. Some know that they have it and have never physically hurt a child.

Post-Traumatic Syndrome

As young as I can remember, I knew God. I can only remember from the day that I met Larry, the day that he got into our VW in 1970. He got into our car, and said to me, "Hello, sexy," and I knew he was bad and I was in deep trouble. And I was. I remember him hanging around my mom and waiting to get to me. He had long hair, surfer, guitar player, and he had a zig zag tattoo on his upper arm. He was six foot, 2 inches, and he had a long beard, too. My mom had no clue who she opened her palace up to. As he waited to get to me, I could feel a type of hyperness, I would say. I was bouncing more. I felt like I was becoming ready for combat, and who the fuck is going to believe me?

I would like to tell my story for all people, not just other sexual slaves, survivors, but all people who have had trauma to their nervous system and their loved ones and friends, what we as people go through with PTSD and how it affects all of us. The wretched pain that many people go through can take you to places of many, one place you can go is to the child molester's world that is if you have PTSD from sexual abuse, or maybe it's a gift and you can't explain it to people. They don't have the info that your brain has or anything that comes from being a survivor of any trauma of the nervous system, similar to an octopus's nervous system. Octopuses like to taste their environment and who they come across. They feel

12

everything through their nervous system and it's on the outside. It's thick through their skin. It feels like you can read body language very well, and you smell it, taste it, hear it, and feel it. I realize that it just isn't always what you think it is, or feel. That's not to say that you're never right, but you can be sure that most people don't understand or have a care about it because they don't think about it, until they have lived it: sexual abuse and the monster trapped inside.

With this type of monster, you won't comprehend, but I can only give clues to help you, and it's up to you to understand it or to get it, so to speak. When you grow up with certain things, like visiting your grandparents, who loved you and took very loving care of you, and were grateful to have grandchildren because they're the next generation to carry on those bodies and genes, and DNA. If you have grown up giving blow jobs or getting forced for years to have your mom's boyfriend lick on your vagina with a scruffy beard, and who is physically and mentally abusive to your entire family, or if you have had to have sex with your mother or father your whole life, then you learn about these kind of characteristics and you know their every move, their facial expressions, their words, moods, anger, what they want and feel at all times. They are your master. This is not the kind of master you like. This is the kind of master you might want to attack or have a plot to get them, just like in that really good movie, "Matilda" where her family abused her and she got special powers and was able to shut the bedroom door and lock it, where she's sitting on the bed because of her energy.

The funny thing about it is that there are many kinds of this species and there are males and females both. Unfortunately, even the best can be tricked. That's why we must be on our guard for our yard. We have to have a safe place that pedophiles who have opened up and become honest, and who have not acted on their desires, for them to come out of their closet, so to speak, so they are not bullied.

I have just recently started to understand the female child molester. I have met a few. When I talk about a little gal in her thirties that I met at the mental hospital I was 44 at the time, when I went into the mental hospital for the first time. She was my first person that I ever met that had been molested by a female child molester for her entire life. (No, I take that back, I met one other in a sexual survivor group in my late twenties.) The sweet young lady that I met my first time in the mental hospital had been molested from birth to the age of fourteen or fifteen by her mother, for years and years. She is the one that I have talked about that makes squeaking noises, and her nervous system is constantly rotating like an electricity line. She ran obsessive-compulsively 25 miles a day, and had to live in a home, and was on Disability. Her nervous system was like a glowing light. I loved her, and I still do, and I would sit with her and give her as much time as I could while I was in there getting help for myself. She was skinny as a rail and she would put everything on her plate really plain. She would throw up after eating. I love her from head to toe, even though she'll never know. She may have felt it that day, the thirty days that I was there, and the after day treatment that the mental hospital put me in.

The male I know, I know a few of the types that lurk. I have met several, and before I get into these different types, I just want to make it clear that this is from my own life experiences and of years of turmoil and running into them. Although I have saved many children, it will never be enough. I know it sounds a little fetishy (the Slayer). I am still learning but there are a few that I can talk about. I'm very new at explaining my nervous system, so please bear with me. And for those who have had this much or more experience, please be careful with yourself. Often, but not always, the male species has a look about them, a lost look, a daze. My father told me this. It's a twinkle in the eye, a non-existence, a lost little boy or girl, with a lot of sadness, anger, and humiliation. Another way to look at it would be 80% animal and 20% human. Hunger, a deep hunger, a loss of consciousness of their behaviors, a deep desire for a sexual encounter, just like a vampire who has chosen the blood of humans. Lost in a non-developed mind, a mind of only sexual control, can they control this? No. Do they understand it is wrong and they are hurting others? Some do, but that won't be enough to change, only death can stop this species. I once met a man in his early thirties who openly admitted at a job interview with me that he was in trouble with pedophilia and he stopped doing it. He was regressing as he was talking to me to a younger age. He did not realize how aware I was of his behaviors, but he openly admitted it, and said that he stopped and isn't doing it anymore. Ha ha – that's funny as fuck. I'm not making fun of him, it's just when you know something, it's funny to sit there and watch people bullshit right through it, you have to realize and come to the grips that you can't fix them. (I once heard a saying that goes like this, like assholes, we all have an opinion. What I am trying to say is that this is my observation and opinion from what I saw growing up and all of the experience that I have had time and time again. This is not to say that medication could subside the feelings, possibly, but it will be up to the perpetrator to take them, unless you are watching them take them, and then still it's not a 100% guarantee that it'll control their sexual appetite.) That's not to say that some of these species will come forward and tell the truth and a round-about repent knowing that they will always want to do it, and they will always have it in their minds, but they know that they have to stay away from children, which is very sad for them because they are children themselves, longing to be free of the misery of running around as a non-developed human in their brain. Now of course you will meet people who want to believe they can stop it, but believe me, DOWN DEEP THEY DON'T WANT TO. That is why, down deep, they are going to run into me, the Slayer, the octopus lady because I can't sleep until the children are at peace. I'm talking dead ones and alive ones, from hundreds of centuries.

That's why this type of species must be put down, just like a dog that is suffering and causing others to suffer - one that you can't trust, but that you love so much. Or, should I say, you thought you loved, because they aren't who you thought they were. Because they aren't capable of loving the way that humans love. My stepdad would cry and talk in an 8 year old's voice. You had to be there. He would say, "We shouldn't do this anymore" in a child's voice. By this time, I was nine or ten, and I was a thousand years old by this time, within my soul. I think in the seven year period, he had remorse when he got caught. He even cried at the court hearing when I was at it at 36 and was subpoenaed by the Santa Cruz court system. He cried there. I felt like, what a bunch of bullshit. My give-a-damn button was broken by this time. I knew what I was dealing with, and I knew that I had to put him down. The other girls in the court room, including my sister, and my mother, and his last victim, I was going to make sure for all of us in that court room, that he would never touch another child again or hurt another female again.

This is how the day would start out. Get up, step dad watching TV in his room on his bed (dark gloomy feeling waking up out of bed, knowing what's coming ahead), where his brown circle was on the sheet, that not even bleach could get out. Watching Warner Bros. cartoons, which he ruined for me. I still think they're cool, but they certainly do trigger the memory every time. I have learned to let it pass for the most part, when it comes up. Most of the day, then he would be happy as long as he had sexual gratification, sexual games all day, at breakfast, lunch, dinner, and snack. Certain days would be extra scary and ugly, but as soon as he felt loved, his deep sexual feasting, he would be normal for a period of time. What I mean by normal is that he would give me some free time; he would give me rewards, like ice cream at Thrifty's, guaranteed. Going to church, not guaranteed, unless I did it all perfect, all week. He would buy candy to put on his privates as a way of rewarding me. He felt that he owned me and I was his possession. Most of his time was spent on me, and some on my sister, as well as any new kid that I would bring over, except for my best friend of 42 years and her little sister. (I never told my best friend that I was being abused, and she was in my life from when I was nine years old, when I just got off the plane from Maui. Maui wowee.) My best friend is still in my life today. Even in the late night, he would come into my bedroom and do sexual things to me, and slap my face and wake me up. When you are laying there as a child, scared, because you know it's coming and he slaps you as hard as he can across the face, and tells you that if you ever tell again, he is going to kill you and your family. Then I had to get up and go to school the next day. Fuck.

You could sea the urgency and desperation and anger through him until he was sexually gratified by ejaculation. Similar to craving it, or jonesing for it, I pointed this out before. Total personality change.

16

Disgrace
You pissed yourself off
And blamed me.
You cried to the moon and
Back and then laughed in
My face with disgrace on
Your face, why, oh why, do
You blame me.

You can't think you are in control anymore. You have no control over your own life anymore. It lingers through your nervous system even when you are not at home, and at school. You are still under the control of the pedophile. That's why you feel like you want to take him down.

Some other things that my step dad would do all the days and nights is smell my underwear, and he would always ask me to wash my private parts every time before he would lick them. He would ask me to get a warm wash cloth. At this time, I would do what he would say without the ability to complain or say no about it. It was just what he wanted. He would be so mean to my family and I couldn't bear it, so I just did it. Meaning, my mom and my sister would have to endure his mean personality. Meaning, don't rock the boat. ("It's easier to trick somebody than it is to convince somebody that they are being tricked." - Mark Twain)

Larry would sometimes complain about his mother being very mean and degrading and shoving his head down the toilet and getting mad at him because he would be with his sister in the bath tub. They weren't that different in age. She would say, "Don't look at your sister." And he would get into trouble. He never said much else about his childhood. He would say it to me often, though.

My fifth grade year is the year that Larry was very into wanting to marry me. I remember thinking, it's never going to happen, dude.

I was held back in Kindergarten. When I first met Larry is when I started Kindergarten. I got lucky to be able to go to Kindergarten, first, and second grade on the Island of Hawaii. I was held back my first attempt at Kindergarten. Larry was always there from my first time to Kindergarten to sixth grade.

My grandmother, later in my life, admitted that she and my family knew all along. Those thoughts keep racing through my mind. I guess that's why they call it PTSD.

I remember my mom having a hard time. She had me at a very young age, and us girls love our baby daddies. We almost will do anything for them, including giving up our own children. I know not everybody does this. There are some very strong mothers and fathers out there, that are phenomenal parents, and they make me feel such joy, and I am so happy when I come across some of them. But let's not get astray of the ones that really need us.

I learned to adjust to the fear of feeling trapped. It was cloudy and sunshine at the same time, almost like you have an anxiety to get something done and you can't procrastinate because of the consequences. That's what kept me on my toes to take care of Larry's needs. I had a job to do and I got it done. We always try to make our scary monsters happy so that our day can go better. We have to go to school and act like everything is normal. We have to act like everything is normal around other friends and family. We don't want to get in trouble. I would get in trouble for all of them. I thought that I could handle it. They were so scared, they could barely do anything. I could control the pedophile with a special trick, and I was able to protect my family. My family is the Golden Pearl Army, and I am the leader of the army. I will admit it, it was getting harder and scarier and more deep for him. He wanted to get married and start a family; I wanted to get the fuck out of there.

Larry hated gay people, and I loved all people. He always would say how bad and weird they were, but I remembered how nice they were to me. Not like him, not even a comparison. They were loving, normal people, like my cousin. Larry's brain was centered at all times on his sexual desires. He would drill my head with how bad gay people were, and I remember myself thinking, "Shut the fuck up, you dumb fuck." Sorry about that.

The pain of losing people you love is far above all painfulness and when you can't trust many, it can be a very painful lifestyle. When life is full of letdowns from man or whether it be a woman, we can't give up. We have to feel that pain and embrace it as best we can when we are trapped and really, there is no way out. Losing yourself is a horrific tragedy when you are a slave to your environment, when you are all chained up and there is no way out, everywhere you look, there is no hole, crack, or walkway, or even a chance. There it is, right in front of you. You know that they'll be back for you. You won't be able to win. You are broken. After the master cowards you down, you are so down, you don't even know you're down. It becomes a routine. My God, come quickly. He told me that he is on his way, when I turned to him when I was a child. But I still had to endure the scary days and nights of a very sick man with no end in sight. How they capture their nest as they groom their prey and all they capture. When you go through those rooms and you stay in them, it sometimes takes hours, days, weeks, when you are living with this type of species that has taken you over.

The Golden Layered Onion:
The Bittersweet Pain of Post-Traumatic Stress Disorder
The Journal of a Child Sex Slave
April 12, 2016

My name is Cidney Dawn Anderson. I was born on Nov. 5, 1965 to parents who had just turned 17, prior to my birth. My father was a drug addict. By the age of two, I had already sean Led Zeppelin in concert. We lived in hotels along the coast of California – Orange County. My father was a very violent man, and he was abusive, his mother was abused by my grandfather physically for many years. My father grew up with an abusive father who used to tell him that he was stupid and would never be anything. Although my grandfather I'm sure loved his son, he pounded in his head negative thoughts hoping that it would have reverse psychology on him. Instead, he just reproduced another one of him, violent. My real father never sexually abused me or my sister. He never hurt us on a physical level, but he did hurt us by what he did to my mother and how he would leave us, and we would be on our own a lot.

My mom worked for the airline – Douglas Aircraft. One day, she took a drive to visit my father, in Canada. She was a very jealous person – anybody would be if they got pregnant at 16 and then had two babies. Being the jealous young 20 year old that she was, she got in a Volkswagen and drove to Canada. By this time, I was four and a half years old. We were looking for my real dad and when we got to Canada, we got ahold of him and he introduced us to his best friend's younger brother, Larry. My mom, being the jealous person that she was, tried to make my father very jealous, so when Larry got into the car, little did she know that he wasn't interested in her at all. He was interested in me. He turned to me, and he said, "Hello, sexy." And, even then, at the age of four and a half, I knew how wrong he was, even at that young age, I thought "Oh, fuck." Nobody else in the car knew, but I did. He was there just to get to me. At that age, it's hard to put into words what is wrong about someone; you can feel it, but it's hard to tell somebody else. **The day-to-day grind of my 24-hour day.**

My mom was the vindictive 20-year old girl who tries to get the boy who got her pregnant jealous. So, she hooked up with Larry, who she actually ended up marrying.

My mom would go to work at 7 or 8 in the morning. From 8 a.m. in the morning, I would be running around the house naked, with my little sister, and Larry would babysit us all day long. He didn't work because he would become very jealous of where I was at, and what I was doing while he was at work. Then he would become very violent, festering in his thoughts of me and where I am at and what the fuck I am doing. As the days went on when he did work, he got angrier and angrier. He would be more interested in me making him breakfast than my mother, even at seven. So my mom would go to work and let this boyfriend of hers watch her two daughters all day long until night when the pizza parlor closed, and then some, too. He would come in at night. And my mom needed a babysitter, so, perfect scenario for Larry.

Basically, all day long, at this age at 5 years old, he would put our feet in his hands, and land our vaginas on his face. He had us grind and ride him. As time goes on, he is taking pictures of us on a day to day basis and then burning them in the back yard. Acts of tying us up from the wooden beams in the garage, naked, then did sexual acts upon my sister and me. He was also abusive to my sister, and even the dog (although not sexually abusive to the dog, just physically).

By the age of 6 or 7, he would try to convince me and my sister on a regular basis that being gay was evil and horrible and bad, even as he was molesting us on a day to day basis. He would drill this into us even as he would have me do sexual gay acts with my sister.

By the age of 7, he would pick his nose and get gigantic boogers and chase me around the house all throughout the day, every day. He wouldn't let me get into the refrigerator unless I gave him a blow job or any kind of sexual favor. He was in control of every move I made. This went on every two to three hours during the 15-hour day my mom would be gone, running our family's pizza parlor. Larry had a night stand, and on his side of the bed, there was a circle, where he always sat. He never got up from there very often. On the side of his night stand he had chocolate candies and sweet and sour sugar sticks that we would sprinkle on him. It was never ever fun. We were allowed to have those and rub them on his dick before sucking him. My sister would cry every fucking time

21

because she didn't want to do it. I would take care of Larry so that she wouldn't have to.

There were games every day up to 11 PM at night, and dancing. He always made me clean my vagina before any sex acts. If I was to go to market for him, if I picked up a cucumber or banana, he would talk dirty to me. He never let go of me; he was always squeezing my boobs. His fetish was to always be squeezing my boobs all day long. He would tell me that squeezing my boobs all day long would make my boobs big when I grow up. I would like to tell you a ballerina coincidence, and it goes like this: I just told my husband that if Larry hadn't squeezed my boobs, I probably wouldn't have had quadruple D's, I probably would have been flat chested like my mother and grandmother and sisters all were. I would have been a famous ballerina. I was telling my husband this in the car and two days later, my dad calls me up and asks if I can come visit, and I said, yes. I went over spontaneously. He gave me a gift and it was a ballerina; a pretty plastic and glass ballerina that I hung in my car.

Pickles were a big thing because I wasn't allowed to eat many things. I could have a pickle, which he made into a sexual thing. At that age, I didn't know it was the pickle that triggered his sexual thoughts. Also, he would always come up behind me while I was lying on my stomach watching TV; so eventually, I stopped lying on my stomach and sat Indian-style. I remember being very aware of my body as a sexual object to him.

He had a jealous side, and he beat me for lying. One time, I had lied to him, and he found out. I was in fifth grade and had a big crush on the 17-year old boy next door. Larry stood there silently while my mother asked me if I went into their bedroom, and Larry had a look on his face like "you are going to fucking get it." My mom told me that if I told the truth, I would not be in trouble. Little did she know that right after she left to the store with my sister, Larry came after me, and he spanked me until I'd tell him, "I love you, daddy. I love you, daddy." I'd have to give him a blow job and sexual play. My mom would come back home and was never told what happened.

Finally I told her it was happening again and she tried to work it out with him, and she made him move out to Santa Cruz. Later, she sent me by myself to visit him in Santa Cruz, at the age of 9. Why didn't I say to my mom, no. It is because I was afraid of Larry to death, and I must have been so co-dependent to pleasing him and my mother, that I'd do anything.

Larry got after me every day for some kind of sexual play, all day, it would occur every single day. He would get angry at me for something or another in order to manipulate me to turn it all around for him to be back on top, pouncing on me. If I wanted to go to a friend's house, I'd have to give him a blow job. I'd have to take care of him before I went out for the night, even in empty apartment buildings. We would sneak into them for sexual acts. He would take me into the apartment complex where my friends lived and he would take me into empty rooms for sex.

By the time I'd get back home, he'd be back on the sexual play right away.

He would come into my room in the night, probably after midnight, because my mother would be exhausted after working 12-13 hour shifts. I'd be exhausted from him abusing me all day long. It would feel as if it were a tight muscle tenseness in your nervous system, almost where you're not breathing a lot, like holding your breath. You stay stuck in that as if your heart is tight. Back then, they would call it uptight or strung out.

The first time that I went into a mental hospital, about ten years ago, I was on the beach a lot, with my full blooded German Shepherd, in my Mercedes station wagon. I was making a lot more money back then, sometimes I would have 12 weddings a week to prepare for. I worked for myself, and I enjoyed my work very much. But pretty soon, I started getting really depressed all of a sudden. So bad that even pot couldn't help it. I started losing desire altogether. I had a $750 car payment. (That was only one car by the way.) I would go to the beach, and I was really friggin' depressed, and I had to fake it every day through all that pain and pressure weighing down on my heart.

I met this 88 year-old lady. We ended up spending about 6 weeks together. I would clean the beach as my therapy and as a gift to the world and to the fish. I would pick up a lot of trash. I met this lady with 4 dogs, who could barely walk. I would sing this song by the Beatles, "The long and winding road that leads to you"...because

I wanted to sea my real father so desperately, who I hadn't sean in years. He is the one who saved me from the predator pedophile Larry.

The Ghosts that Come Through Me:
the Boy in the Picture and Sister Angel

I met this lady on the beach, and one day, she looked at me, and said that I belonged in Oregon. One day, I told her that I was molested, and my mother wouldn't save me. She said, when she caught her husband molesting her daughters who were 12 and 13, and she asked them if he had touched them, and they said, "yes" – she had him out of the house in 15 minutes. My mother wasn't like that. That's when I had a truth come to me – a knowledge – that my mother really did let me down, and what she did was really really bad by staying with him and not protecting me. It was almost like I got a stamp, like a brand, a burn in my heart knowing the truth that my mother had forsaken me. I went into a Post Traumatic trance.

I said that I would go to the store to dig the food out of the trash bins at the market for her so that she didn't have to. Because that is where she'd go to get the food for herself and her dogs. I would get into the bins on Wednesdays for her. I remember feeling like I wasn't in my own body. I realized I had a bigger force than my own running my body to help her. I helped her a lot. One day, I was at her home, and I was looking around her house and I saw that it was really messy. There was a lot of dirt; she was a complete pack rat. I started cleaning and helping her get her kitchen back to normal. I also did her feet; she had really long yellow toe nails, and I did her toe nails. I was in a merciful state for humans.

I saw a picture of a young man on the wall, and he was about 16. I asked her who it was. She said it was her grandson, who shot himself in the head at age 18 because his father had been sodomizing him his whole life. The parents were divorced and the dad had half custody; and his dad abused him for many years at gunpoint. He would be dropped off at his father's house every weekend. The father had no mercy and no remorse, afterwards, he just kept inviting other neighbor boys over. They can't save themselves; we have to stop it; and they won't turn themselves in.

I had an overwhelming feeling come over me. My deep post-traumatic stress came. I went into a trance almost; an overwhelming urgency came over me. I could feel that I was about to go into a dark, dark tunnel. I was being called to help this boy. I told the grandmother and the daughter, when I was sitting at the kitchen table, that I would go to the neighborhood where his dad lived and let the neighbors know since the father got away with it. I would warn the neighbors of the beast living at the end of the street. They could tell that I knew what I was talking about and that the boy was coming through me. She was so happy when I told her what I was going to do. I asked for the address, and she gave it to me, joyfully. She was so lifted from the wretched chains that bounded her and her daughter, that they could maybe do one thing for this angel boy who committed suicide and left a note. As I drove into the cul de sac, and passed the dad's address, I saw a lady watering her front yard at the end of the cul de sac. Me and my German Shepherd drove to the end of the cul de sac and I asked her if she knew about the young man who had shot himself, and she did. I asked her if she knew why he died; and she did not. I told her what happened. She said, thank you very much for telling me, since she had five boys and the father of the teen boy who shot himself would invite them over to play.

The old lady and her daughter were so happy that I did this, since the father that had sodomized his son had gotten away with this crime. I informed the neighbors that he had abused his son, and asked that they pass this information along. I know that the ghost of the young man who shot himself in the head got some closure through what we did for him. I know the family did. True love can always prevail and keep a family and a ghost together.

I'd like to tell another coincidence, maybe it's not a big one to others, but I know that it's a big one for me. Last week, I was shopping at a thrift store and I got an overwhelming feeling. I looked up and I saw a picture for sale for 10 cents. Lately, for the last few months, I have been finding dimes. The gentleman that is 80 that I take care of has told me to make sure that I pick up my dimes. He said that dimes bring you good luck. So, when I looked at the picture, it had a young man on it who looks like he is 18, he has huge angel wings with a guitar in his hands. I knew that it was my friend the ghost boy that I helped him and his family. I know that he is here to help me.

I went into the mental hospital for the first time, about 4 days after driving down the cul de sac. I had to let my little old lady friend know that I was going to be in there. I had a complete breakdown. My mind and body were completely and utterly exhausted. I was crying for days and days without being able to stop at all; it was like a rain storm. I tried everything. I started taking my husband's Tramadols and in a four day period, I had gotten 14 Tramadols in one day. I was slowly killing myself and overdosing. I remember driving myself to the mental hospital while my husband sat in the passenger seat passed out on Codeine and Tramadol, he was coming in and out of withdrawal. He had a stressful job, and worked his ass off. He drove hours and hours to get to work and back. The pain killers got to him, like they do to many people.

I got there, crying the entire way, without being able to stop at all. Tears flowing out without control. We got to the mental hospital and because I took the 14 Tramadols, it looked like a suicide; although it wasn't that. It was helping an energy force – the boy in the picture. When I got there, I realized that I didn't belong there after 2 days. I was in there 3 days total. I noticed that I started helping everybody else that was in there, including the help. I got out of my trauma of the boy in the picture. I came back to reality, and they said that I could get out as long as I went through a 30-day program. Every day for 30 days, I would check into a day unit. I would go to different groups all day long and get a breakfast and a lunch. In my group, I met this young lady whose mother had molested her all of her life. Her PTSD was really bad off, and so were her levels of PTSD. She would make noises all the time while we were sitting in group. She ran almost 25 miles every day and was almost anorexic. I tried to help her, but her mother had molested her for so long that her brain had to shut down partially, almost like a computer when it makes noises. I knew then that God had sent me to her and that I was on another mission in life.

In 2015, I started as a caregiver, and the gal that I worked for was Sister Angel. I got a job with the Department of Human Services. I met her at my church and I was doing service, going to her house and helping her pack. She said that she needed a caregiver, and I needed a job that could support my family. She said to go and make an application, and I could work for her 30 hours a week. I got the job, and started working for Sister Angel, and little did I know, but Sister Angel had a pill problem – she was addicted to opiates. She was 30 years old, with chronic depression and suicidal thoughts. I begged her and told her she was worth so much. I was sorry that she had so many losses. I know it is hard to make it on this planet. But after trip after trip, because she'd take all her prescriptions, so she had to go the ER, I told her that I could no longer be an enabler to her, and I resigned. Then I went into a deep depression where I could not get out of bed. Similar to the depression that I had ten years ago. I tried to help her, but she would not return my calls.

Then I got a job for a family who owned a car lot, and they hired me to take care of their mother. I took the job and I was there for 6 months. One day, the lady that I was taking care of, was in a lot of pain. She got up and said that she had to use the restroom, she was shaking and barely able to walk. She made it to the bathroom, where she went in privacy. I turned my head to the left and looked at the wheel chair in the hall next to me. As I was standing there, staring at the wheel chair, I noticed that it said, "Forever End." It was on the wheel chair. She came out of the bathroom and we went back to her room. But in the hallway, I had an overwhelming feeling pass through me that Sister Angel either died, or was going to die.

I sat down, and I realized that I needed to take pictures of the back of that chair, because I wanted people to know that I wasn't making this stuff up. So, I left work on Sunday afternoon, went home to my husband, and explained to him that Sister Angel either died or was going to die. Tuesday evening, on our way to Karaoke night, we went into the liquor store, and I looked up, and there was Sister Angel's next-door neighbor. He told me that she died on Saturday night. I started crying because I already knew. These are the types of coincidences that occur with me, and I have proof that angels are around us.

The Golden Layered Onion:
The Bittersweet Pain of Post-Traumatic Stress Disorder
The Journal of a Child Sex Slave
April 26, 2016

About three years ago, in 2014, I took all of the California real-estate tests and passed them. I was laying in my room, and I had this overwhelming feeling that I needed to work with children again. I had a pre-school assistant certificate, but I had just signed on at Keller Williams. Even when I was sitting in my car, I felt like I needed to work with kids, which was ridiculous because I had just passed my real estate exam. But it was like I could hear the children crying for help. It almost felt like a fly when you are sleeping that keeps landing on your face, and you try to shush away.

I told my husband that I was not going to be a real estate agent, and I was a little nervous. I had to tell him that I was having a calling and my real estate profession was going to be on hold, and he was willing to let me do whatever I wanted to do. I then knew that I needed go back to working with kids. I put "foster jobs in Oregon" in the computer because my father lived in Oregon. I thought I could do both, be with my father and help children. All of a sudden a job comes up, stating "Must love kids, in Oregon." I decided to call them, but I had no idea where the town was. I had no idea what I was getting my family and myself into. I had a phone interview and I got a job offer. The Director, Mr. Monster, tried to tell me how terribly the kids had been abused. I felt that I had the qualifications to give the children a ray of hope; little did I know…

I was excited to go to Oregon. The ad said, "Must love children." I knew my father was there; and he ended up being only 11 miles away from where I was going. What a coincidence! I went in my PT Cruiser with my whole family. This was within a week of passing my real estate courses. We were on our way to Oregon, for my job interview for a job called "therapeutic foster care parent" for abused children. The job was working with kids who had been taken out of their homes for severe abuse, who were violent in school. I showed up in a 2 piece cream maternity suit that I got at the thrift store. I was interview for months and I had extensive background checks and finally we drove back home to California, packed our bags, and moved into a 6,000 square foot house. The school I was hired at serves children up to 12 years old. The children get sent by the State to this school for having been violent in regular school, or who are in foster care. This school is in the foster care system. Basically, I had three bosses: the State (Department of Human Services), and the Center, as well as the Director.

I had the most dangerous child of the County in my care.

I don't want to blame anybody, but I know what was there. I reported the abuse that I saw and I found out later that others had already reported abuse. I felt alone, with no support as a mandated reporter, I felt scared. I was bullied a lot.

I was hired to work at the Center's Weekend Program called "respite" for foster parents to take their foster children to have a break. The Director and his son ran the respite center, and they hired me and my husband to do that program, as well as being a foster mother and our daughters were volunteers. The bus would come and pick them up. I would be there, cooking and helping run the little class time, as well as playground, and dodge ball. In the teacher's classrooms, on respite weekends, where I started seaing the abuse big time, they were putting them in lock-down – two adults holding one kid down. They told me that I had to be certified for respite, so I would come to classes, but later I came to find out that they were not even certified for it at the time. Also, the type of lockdown was where these children could have heart attacks – it was very hard on these kids. They told me that if I could not hold the kid down, that I could not pass the test. I understood that a kid needs to be restrained from hurting himself, but 2 adults and the kid hyperventilating in a corner in a room. The 2 adults were a little aggressive for the children, and it looked to me like I would never want to have my children in there ever. I don't sea how that can help a child that has been abused heal; I know for a fact that it would not help me heal.

On this week day, the school was closed for the teachers, and the Director was alone with this girl. That day, he let me work, my daughter work, and his son. The school was closed for Easter break, but it was open for respite care. When they did that – he (the Director of the school) abused this girl. I saw him touch the girl's private area, and she mumbled, "Stop." (She was only four and a half.) He didn't know how alert I was to sexual abuse, because he didn't know my background before he hired me. I saw the sexual abuse, and I called DHS to report it. (Little did I know that he had other allegations against him already.) When he was told that he was not allowed to be around the girl for respite anymore; he closed the school down for respite, and called it real day treatment.

I know that I work for the Golden Pearl Army because I am always at the right place at the right time. When I ran into the little girl's mother, she said "thank you" and that they had reported it in the past. All of a sudden, the girl wasn't coming to the respite care anymore.

That is why I came here, and that is my intuition. I came here to help those children.

The Director resigned. I thought he was the bomb initially, but everything he set up was fake. It really depleted me. It took me to a different place in my brain. They bullied me horrifically. It wore me to pieces; especially since there was no support and no help, and it was scary, let me tell you.

I call it the Golden Pearl Army that helps these children when they call for help. It is an army for the children of the land. The leader came to earth to save the human race. I'm here for the Golden Pearl Army, and I have wings -they can call it bi-polar, or whatever they like, but that is how I sea it.

No one believed me and no one understands what it is like to be aware of these particularly sick people, but I sacrificed my own self and my family's well-being without realizing that I was putting my family and myself in danger.

I'm proactive for trans-gender people, and for people who are gay and straight. They are not hurting anyone. They are being honest with their sexuality. I stand up for not hurting people; especially children. Not one single kid likes to be abused.

The 10th Most Wanted Man by the FBI in San Diego and Riverside County

When I was 25, and I was living in Costa Mesa, California. I was in my own wooden cottage, for $950 per month and I was struggling to pay my rent. I started researching the newspaper for a place

that would be cheaper that was a 2 bedroom, so that I could rent a
room out. I saw an ad that said "$750 moves you in." So, I called
the number and was told that I would be shown the apartment by
Mike, the apartment manager. Mike took me upstairs to the apartment, and that's when all of a sudden, I had a black out; I couldn't
move or even look around at the apartment. And, I love homes,
and to look at them and to look around, but I couldn't move. I
looked at Mike and I had an out-of-body experience, I didn't know
what it was at first. Finally, I came back to the apartment and to my
body. I thanked Mike and I left.

I went downstairs and told him that I'd be in touch. I got in my
first cream car, a Honda, it was about 7 p.m., and I adjusted my
rear view mirror, and there is Mike, grabbing a five year old boy's
pants, and shoving a hose down the back side of them. I panicked,
and tried to calm myself down, I told myself that just because you
were abused doesn't mean that everybody is getting abused; you're

panicking, Cidney. At the time, I didn't know that I had PTSD, although I was told by my wonderful therapist of thirty eight years. She warned me of this thing we call PTSD. I left and went home. I decided not to go back to those apartments since it put me in such a depression for 3 to 5 days, to where it was like I couldn't move. Then one day, I looked at an ad, about 2 weeks after the visit with Mike, I saw an ad that said "$750 moves you in." I told myself that I was imagining it, and that Mike was not a pedophile, and that I would be okay.

So, I called the ad up again, and the owner answers the phone again, and I told him that I don't have the first or last months' rent, and he said that I only needed to pay $350 now, and when I find a room-mate, the rest can be paid. I could move in now. Wow – what a deal!

I went to the apartment and moved in. One day, I had an appointment with my therapist, and I had to be there at 1 o'clock, so I left at 12:30 in the afternoon. I passed all of the other apartments, and Mike's was last on the left. When I came to where Mike's apartment was, his door was open; he was sitting there with no shirt on, with a boy who is about 12 years old, who is also sitting with no shirt on. This was a school day. I asked Mike why the boy was out of school, and he said that he didn't have school today. I continued to leave for my appointment feeling my heart racing rapidly.

I went into dark post-traumatic stress again – I finally got to my counselor's office. How I got there, I don't know. I proceeded to tell my therapist that this boy was being molested as we speak in my apartment complex. She tried to calm me down, and asked me, how do you know? My body almost like it was going in reverse, with the wind sucking me in reverse, with my hair flowing forward because it's so strong and fast. After she asked me that, I explained to her in detail the environment and the crime scene.

I get home and pull into the apartment complex, and I look up and Mike's front door is shut and his curtains are closed. His car is there, so I know that he is home. So, I go upstairs to his apartment and knock on the door, and he doesn't come to the door for at least a minute, maybe longer; it felt like a lifetime. It's a very small apartment. He comes to the door with a towel around his neck, no shirt on, and just a pair of jeans. I asked him what took him so long, and where is the boy? He said, "He's in the bedroom watching videos. What's wrong, are you having a fight with your boyfriend?" I went into Post Traumatic Shock again, because I had the same wind again, pulling me in reverse, through a tunnel. It sucked me back to reality.

I went home and called 911, and I told them that my neighbor was molesting a boy. A cop knocked at my door within 3 to 4 minutes of my call. I told him to get away from me since he would blow my cover.

The cop goes to Mike's door, and Mike had hidden down the stairs in a vacant apartment – since he was the apartment manager, he had all of the keys. When the cops went to the door, the kid said that he didn't know where Mike was. Mike was paying him, since he was a runaway. The cop left since he could not find Mike.

So, I come out of my apartment. Mike comes out of the empty apartment downstairs. I told him,

"If there are going to be any cops here, I don't want to live here." This was to deflect suspicion that it was me who had called the cops.

One day when Mike was gone, and I was at home, two 11-12 year old boys (including the same boy) come walking past my apartment. So, I called out to them to come to me, and they did. I made up a story that I wanted to go fishing but I didn't know how, and I asked for their number, so that I could call their mothers. I spoke with one of the boy's mothers, and I told her that her son is being molested. Mike pays for their movies, and then he takes them back home with him. I know this because I asked the boy, and he told me. I told the mother that if she is going to the movies, Mike will sea her, and run away.

I had been living there 2 weeks. That night, the cops come again, and Mike wasn't home again. At the time, I was working as a waitress, and I had to take a leave of absence because I had a breakdown. I got a job where Mike worked (he also worked as a telemarketer in addition to being the apartment manager). Finally, I go back to my work as a waitress and I get a call at 5:30 a.m., that the cops are taking Mike away in hand-cuffs. They got him on his hands and knees.

He ended up being the 10th most wanted man by the FBI, in

33

San Diego and Riverside County. He got 12 years.

They made me a hero of the year, and hero of the month.

That was an exhausting 3 weeks in that apartment. What a coincidence.

Then I got to move into my bestest place. 2nd Street down town H.B!

That was one of my big validations that I have a gift.

My ex-boyfriend has the article. The Daily Pilot – Costa Mesa, California – it happened around 1991. I don't know Mikes last name.

The Golden Layered Onion:
The Bittersweet Pain of Post-Traumatic Stress Disorder
The Journal of a Child Sex Slave
May 4, 2016

I have been married for many years. My nervous system is still going up and down from working with the Center and being tricked.

Bi-polar may be what it looks like to the medical field.

My nervous system has been over-stimulated and fried.

Example:

In some non-physical world that I lived in, the Director tricked me beyond any way that anyone has ever tricked me. When I took the job, I had been fighting for my husband's life for the past 10 years from a codeine addiction. Mr. Monster tricked me so amazingly – I did believe in this man's work like nobody's business. But when I witnessed the grooming he was involved with, is when my post-traumatic started kicking in. When you sea all of this going on – it's like BAM all of the puzzles clicked. Like you are all alone in a war and in a battle, and you can sea it happening all around you. That snapped it. I was like HOLY SHIT! Once I had to tell 2 different men that they weren't allowed to be in the bathroom alone with the boys. It never occurred to me that Mr. Monster was a molester. I believed in him, and in all of the stories he told me. It hurt – there he was like a vampire, right before my very eyes.

I am a slayer of pedophiles by nature. I have a gift to catch pedophiles.

Once the puzzle clicked, we were at the Center, and that's when I pulled my husband aside, and took him into the nurse's office, and I told him that I was going to get into black tunnels - it is the biggest black hole of pedophiles that I have ever sean. When I looked into my husband's eyes, I could feel myself slowly being sucked out through a tunnel and I only had so much time left. That's when I told my husband that he can either deal with me or get the fuck out and run, because I am not going to be the same person at all. As I slowly lost myself, I did not want to sea my husband get hurt in this battle between me and this other spiritual world.

It was like a karate move in my head – doing a karate act to strike pedophiles coming at you like zombies. Because there are so many, and small grooming, including kids being alone in the bathroom with an adult (which is a big no-no); or in the car alone with an adult (also not acceptable). I walked into a fucking mess of pedophiles.

I get myself into situations – this is like a spiritual level, too – the wings that I have from having lived with a pedophile for so long as a kid. If I had protection, I could be a detective in that division.

I didn't like it, and it scared the hell out of me, so I reported it. As a mandated reporter, I did my job, those kids felt wretched and begged for help.

Within a week I got fired.

In between this time, I got 2 letters from the Director dropped off on my doorstep – begging me, and telling me how good I'm doing, and if there are any problems, this and that. Five or six days later, I was fired.

When I get to the Center initially, I did not know that I was there on a mission for God and the Golden Pearl Army. I said out loud to myself, "Mary, Mary, quite contrary, why am I here?"

Every appliance in the Center's kitchen was broken. The toaster oven / the microwave / the coffee pot – all of it was broken because of some sort of short circuit, and it was real. This was before I knew that there were pedophiles. Nothing in there worked.

That group of people had to accept that Mr. Monster was a bad guy; he was not who they thought he was, or was he? He resigned a week after I reported him. I ran into him at the stores, and I feel so sad. He hurt me and put me in so much mental stress and pain.

He would always tell me, people got my back, people owe me favors. When he called me one afternoon, and said, why do you got to look at the bad stuff? I felt so scared.

Once, when I was a kid, I stood up on the toilet paper roll in my Mom and Larry's bathroom. I did it because I was trying to sea the boy next door. When I was asked, I said, "Yes, I broke it." I knew that I was going to get it. I knew that Larry knew that I was climbing up there to sea the boy next door. So, I stayed home to take the beatings. I had to live in that scared fearful place, knowing that's where your scary monster wants you to stay. That no one was coming for me, feeling as if no one will ever come for me. Larry was going to come in any minute and get me. Sure enough, he came in and he dragged me by my hair. He spanked me and whipped me. I kept apologizing, and then I had to give him a blow job, and everything went back to normal. He became "nice" again. When my mom and sister came home, they never knew what happened.

So for me to know that I was going to get a whipping for reporting the Director – I was ready. I didn't even care; I was oblivious to what might happen to myself. I wanted to make sure the kids were safe. Doing my job like all other good samaritan do at your local grocery store.

It's been a blessing or a curse / I don't know which one we want to call it.

But the last 2 cases have been the worst, because I've been chased.

It's like being a boulder tossed into the water; making a big splash.

The Golden Layered Onion:
The Bittersweet Pain of Post-Traumatic Stress Disorder
The Journal of a Child Sex Slave
May 10, 2016

I lived in Hawaii for a 2.5 year period with my family.

I would steal food because I didn't want to go home to Larry until the last minute. My Mom worked in a burger joint, and was in school full time. So, she was gone a lot.

Larry started to break me because he had been with me since I was five, and now I was seven. He was on me friggin' constantly. By the age of 9 or 10, I'd steal candy bars from the market and sell them to all of the kids in the neighborhood, and I got caught.

That's when Larry was doing drugs and moving marijuana around 1972 to 1974, from Maui to Cali.

I was on the street at my cousin's house, barely making it. I had a break from Larry for about a month. Out of a 7.5 year period, I was lucky to have a 3 month break from his child molesting (the break was spread out over the 7.5 years). We would tell Mom about the abuse, and then we would all forgive him and have him back. My mother wanted him to babysit, and I felt guilty for her financial stress.

Do you want to know the way to San Jose?

We moved from Costa Mesa to San Jose. We got a house two doors down from my mother's best friend.

My grandpa, etc., asked my mother to come and open a pizza parlor. So, I was left with Larry. I remember my mom sitting on the edge of my bed, and me crying and begging her not to leave, but she had already bought her ticket, so I was left alone with Larry for what seamed like a lifetime, but was maybe a week or two. It was like being in a burning hell; it was scary – the house was empty, except for the beds; and I'm alone with this m-fucker, and there were tomato plants in the back yard with big green caterpillars, and I would go there to get out of the house. The caterpillars saved the day; I remember consciously looking at the green caterpillars in the back yard, and Larry coming outside to get me to take care of him. From that moment on, I go into a blackout for a little while.

My mother left me there; I cried when she left. At the time, I probably told her, "It's okay, Mom, I'll be alright." I was so scared of Larry, and the constant sexual games.

The 2 weeks were up and we moved, but it felt like a living hell. I always forgave my mother. I had some kind of fantasy that I was protecting her; or doing it for her as a warrior. I was little and barely hanging on.

My mother walked in on me giving Larry a blow job. It was real. There it was in her face; she couldn't deny what was happening. She saw me on my knees. There it was. There was the truth – it prevailed. The back-up, my sister, watching the back door, failed her job. Larry told her to go watch the door and let us know if mom comes home. She let her walk right on in. So, then we had to get Larry out of the house without getting too bad of a beating.

So, we got out that day.

A week goes by and we are still not back with Larry from that day that my mother walked in. He stayed in the house, and we got out. We went to a hotel for a couple of days. I was in 4th grade, and we had just got back from Hawaii. We only lived in that apartment for about 3 months.

Another time, during that week, I told my mom what happened. She got so mad that she called him on the phone from the hotel room that we were staying at. She said that I want you to tell Larry what you just told me. He admitted it all. My mom was so pissed off; she was pissed off at him and she was pissed off at us. At the whole circumstance, not necessarily caring for us. She said that she was sorry that this had happened. I forgave her and everything. We decided to let him move back in with us – we got a house. Then he did it again; he had to move out again. He moved to Santa Cruz.

So, my mother asked me if I would mind seaing him. She put me on an airplane and sent me to sea him alone. Because he was our stepdad – our daddy. He lived in a cold trailer.

I was so scared that he was going to try something on me. I had hoped he would be getting better. When it came time to go to bed, he was on me like glue. I had a black out for a little while. Back on the airplane going home. My mother just couldn't wait to get rid of me. Thinking back, the whole thing is so evil and so bad and fucked up.

I was possessed by him – for real.

39

Then he came back. We moved into a house – in Huntington Beach. I was in fifth grade. I wasn't allowed in the refrigerator at all, ever. This is a big deal; Larry always wanted control over me. When you tell kids that they can't have food, it's very bad. I learned that from the foster children because they are away from comfort, and food can be very comforting. You can seduce or control kids with food; and that is one of the ways that pedophiles do what they do. I always wanted my foster children to feel like they could eat when they wanted to, and go into the refrigerator and make their own food. I wanted them to feel like they were a part of a group. Mi casa is your casa.

We moved into a 4 bedroom house, and that's when Larry told me that he wanted to marry me. That was when Saturday Night Fever came out – I had a poster of John Travolta above my bed. I had Larry after me 24/7.

In his mind, my sister could join in, but in actual attraction; he was very attracted to me.

My sister would cry so much at that time of each day – four or five times a day of sexual play. She would get very upset at that time. So, I would just do it for her. It's just that he would tell me weird things.

When my real father took me out to dinner at 10 years old; I was telepathically begging him to save me. He was a drug addict, so I didn't sea him much. Like every two years. But we had pizza parlors so that was how he could get a hold of us.

My dad didn't know until he saw the signs at the dinner table at Maxwell's on the pier at Huntington Beach, we met there for dinner. Larry sat right by me, and I sat right next to my real father, Billy. Larry was very controlling over me. I stared at my Dad, deep into his eyes, and I begged him to help me. Within a 2 year span, out of nowhere, my Dad told my mom that Larry is messing with his girls, and if she doesn't call the police on him, he will.

Larry decided to go on vacation to sea his brother Jack who was best friends with my Dad. They were frying on LSD and doing it in the bathroom; Larry was doing that with my Dad. My Dad said, I know you are messing with my girls and you better get the fuck out of here, before I hurt you. The next day, my mother got a call from my real dad, Billy, and he told her to get Larry out now, or I will have you arrested for allowing this.

My mother came over to the couch, and told me that Larry is in trouble. She was angry at us, and me especially. It was at least one year since I saw Bill at Maxwell's and for him to pull his own bootstraps up to get this done.

The police took us in separate rooms and questioned us; we told them everything. Then Larry found out all of the things we had said.

He had me so seduced as a father figure (like, I'll get my ass kicked if I don't do what he wants), that I would call him once to sea how he was doing in the mental hospital or in jail.

He got around 2 years in a mental hospital, and 3 years in jail. He got out of jail when I was 18.

Years later, they subpoenaed me and my sister to testify about what Larry had done to us for all those years. When you get three strikes you're out. Later on, there was a second girl; and then a third girl that he abused – the one sitting in the court room.

The third girl was very bad off – she was seduced by Larry, so she had a feeling of him as a boyfriend; of someone who loves her - she was 12.

I got to tell Larry whatever I wanted – I was 36 at this point, and had a newborn baby in my arms. I stood up for children's rights because children are human beings. They're not yours to whip around, or use for your sexual pleasure; etc. You can love and take care of them, or you can't be around them.

At 36, when I testified, I was so happy to be able to help this girl. I told Larry that he made me go through hell, and sex stuff, and told him that because of what he had done to all of these children, he'll never sea his real daughter (that he had with my mom).

The judge said to Larry, I don't know why you do this, but apparently you cannot stop, you get 42 years to life, with no chance of parole. Larry got 42 years in prison. That was a beautiful day. It was a gift.

I put myself in therapy because I was seductive to men. I knew how to seduce a man very good – any of them. I knew that wasn't healthy; I knew that's not what I wanted to be. I don't want to hurt

41

anybody, or be out of control, so I put myself into therapy; it took me 3 to 5 years to even cry. I wouldn't blame my mother for any of it. My therapist started helping me, and I went to her for 20 years. She knows me inside and out.

The Golden Layered Onion:
The Bittersweet Pain of Post-Traumatic Stress Disorder
The Journal of a Child Sex Slave
May 17, 2016

I no longer need religion; and it's invigorating to figure it out. I know that I'm not going to hell. I have a great relationship with God. I am a member of the Golden Pearl Army. I know it sounds ridiculous, but that's that. I know there are other dimensions. I can sea God, and I know he is there, and then I realized I do love religion, and when you do something religiously you change.

I have too much evidence that God lives.

It doesn't mean it's necessarily a heaven or a hell.

One time, I was at the Mormon Church, and they teach going to the Temple and rituals for the dead.

I was using my body to baptize people who were dead.

I could go to them (the dead) in my soul and connect to them.

In Church, in a room in my Temple Recommendation course, a veil was lifted and I had a vision of a whole bunch of men. I wasn't on any medications or drugs. It was like I was seaing it within myself. I swear that it was real. There was a woman in the Temple course, who was crying a lot. I felt really sympathetic towards her because of her separation from her husband over religious beliefs. The course is for husband and wife to be sealed for eternity.

Another ritual was a patriarchal blessing; the man giving the blessing to me said that I was a leader of Zion, and that all of the children of the church will look up to me. Kids look up at me and smile at me.

One day, I went to pick up my daughter at her friend's house. The friend's little sister ran across the room and gave me a big hug even though she didn't know me. It's because I work for the Golden Pearl Army and they can feel that. Children look up to me and feel safe around me, they know that they are not in danger. So, how do we trust? What are some of the things that a camp could have that you know you have safety? It could be that you're a little girl coming from a background of Cowboys and Indians with a step-parent. Or it could be that I'm going to camp and I'm getting away from that situation. I'm trying to show two ways that it could be happening. Like I said, children do trust and pedophiles can be sneaky and groom your child right before your eyes. Even I have been tricked.

I don't want to call these "blessings" but messages – almost kind of like for real, that I left messages to myself along the way already. So, if I called them blessings then that means that I'm referring to Jesus, but I'm not. I'm not against Jesus; to me, he was a man who suffered for what he believed in very much. And I relate to that. And I have kneeled down to that; and I gave my all to that. I'm already past the churches now; I'm past the level of the church; we create our universe. I only serve my Father God through Jesus Christ.

When I caught the tenth most wanted man by the FBI, and I had my first encounter with the Golden Pearl Army within myself, I got extremely validated by circumstances that were so powerful and amazing, and they touched me with golden pearl dust all over me.

My husband was making good money, and I was running a wedding business. I had anywhere from 5 to 12 weddings a week. My husband was taking anywhere from 15-20 Vicodin, or Percocets.

So, when I moved to Odessa, TX, I woke up one day on a Thursday. I was losing it. My husband is on all of those pills. Thursday morning I wake up and that evening, I tell my husband, we are moving to Odessa, TX.

I ended up literally getting into one of my mental awarenesses where I'm a gypsy. My family had no clue where we were going and why. My husband had family there (his dad), and we loved it there, and the hospitality there. We moved there within 3 days. On the record, I have moved my family around 20 times.

Why I had to go to Odessa: I had already been Mormon for 4 years when we moved there. It was about time to baptize the 2 youngest kids.

So, we get there, we move in, and all of a sudden, I am going to this Presbyterian Church. I walked into the Church's kitchen and I told this older man that I would like to volunteer there. It's like I am walking through a veil again – that dimension that I am there as planned. He hands me the skeleton key of the entire church, and I hadn't even been there a month. He had been in the kitchen for the past 40-50 years there. He starts showing me the kitchen. He has everything labeled in that 1940's kitchen; remodeled in

44

maybe 1960. He has pots and pans hanging from the ceiling. One day, we're in there, he opened up the refrigerator door, and I had a feeling that he would be dying soon. I was like, it's okay, and I can handle this.

I made this friend and she owns pharmacies. We met and became close friends. She went to the Presbyterian Church. She had very expensive bottles of wine parties. One day we were sitting in the Presbyterian cafeteria, and I felt like she would not think that I was off my rocker so I told her that I get messages. I asked her if she saw that man. I said that he is going to die soon and nobody knows it yet. I got the message, and that's why I'm here. He died within 1-2 months of brain cancer; a really quick death. I was his rescue and his friend in the kitchen. It was like I was being trained by him. After only knowing me for 30 days, he gave me the skeleton key to the entire Presbyterian Church.

I became very close to my friend. She had a big thing to do at funerals at the Presbyterian Church. There were a lot of funerals all of a sudden. I went to one of them early, set the whole funeral up, but she never showed up. She forgot the whole funeral. I covered it. It was by the chance of God sending me a miracle to help her.

They asked me to be a deacon in the Presbyterian Church. Unfortunately, I had to turn it down. I had other things to do, and I had already done what I needed to do for them. There were three ladies that were desperately lonely - I had to visit these people. All that they had was the dinners to look forward to.

Within a year of living in Odessa, I sold all of my wedding stuff, and opened my own café.

In Odessa, there are many people like my grandma's age. There are estate sales. I would walk in the rooms of the estate sales. I went to an estate sale one day, and it was a big, 2 acre property, that the person was leaving after being there for 50 years. They had to get rid of stuff. They had these metal barrel drums; they were blue and white. I bought six of them: 3 blue and 3 white. I told my husband that I have to have those barrels. I loaded them up and bought them. I arrived at a "T" stop sign; there was a sidewalk, and I thought, how bitching would those barrels be on the front of my property at the "T". So, I put all six of them at the front of the yard. I was going to put rocks and plants in them, and have it look like a really bitching front yard. The house had a little Italian flair to it.

One night, I decided that my husband and I were going to move our bedroom into the sunroom and make it a bedroom. And then the kids could have the other two bedrooms. We were cramped.

About a week later, after we were all set up in the sun room, our back wall was so pretty, because it was all brick. We put our headboard up against the brick because it looked good.

One night we were sleeping and all of a sudden, out of nowhere, I woke up. It was about 15 seconds and then I got on my knees, and I rubbed my husband's back a bit. It was around 4 in the morning. In the middle of the night, I woke up and tried to wake my husband up. Within 30 seconds, a car hit the house! A girl ran the stop sign, she was going 70 miles an hour; she was on meth and alcohol. She hit the white barrel, which made her swerve just enough so that I could live. I got us both up. Isn't it extraordinary that my body could feel the energy that the car was coming? There are energies that we can be in tune to, especially the more broken you are; so I have some sort of extraordinary gift.

Within one month, I got a check for the brick wall, and I really needed that money for my husband to pay some debts for his heavy drug use of opiates and just other bills we had.

So, that white barrel saved our life. The last time I saw a white barrel was when they dropped white and blue barrels in front of me while I was cycling. That message came to me. I know how it went. Beware of barrels coming your way for later. They dropped barrels in front of my car again.

The man that wrote Tom Sawyer – Mark Twain – came to me. Not through a body. He came to me through a few things. At first, I didn't think a big thing about it. In that story - kids don't run away from loving families. In my opinion, he was trying to teach us about little kids.

Last year, I was taking care of some clients – and I usually am an angel for people close to the end. I am somehow helping people before they leave the earth. You can call it humanitarian, but it gets real deep.

With Mark Twain, I bought this bumper sticker – I never knew he wrote "Tom Sawyer." I bought this bumper sticker that said, "It's easier to trick somebody than it is to convince them that they are being tricked." That was a saying by Mark Twain. That man came through with those words for me at a time when nobody wanted to help those kids. It was like creepy crawlies everywhere – another side that wants to corrupt. Mr. Monster had tricked so many people. This sounds dumb but it was very much like the universe was sending me some gold dust of validations, coming out of the woodworks. Recharging me to keep going.

I got to my client's house, and that was when I had the intuition of Sister Angel.

I was there to help this elderly lady – she was 93. She helped an animal zoo, with lions and giraffes, and was on the Animal Kingdom back in the 1970's and 1980's. She is making me sit there, and I am hyper. All I could do was listen to the books she played, and pick up a book from the shelf. One of the books that I picked up was the biography of Mark Twain. It was almost in a time ball shell that came to me.

The Golden Layered Onion:
The Bittersweet Pain of Post-Traumatic Stress Disorder
The Journal of a Child Sex Slave
May 24, 2016

My mom and Larry were flying back and forth from California to Hawaii with pot. My mom was in her early twenties in Hawaii.

When I got back from Hawaii, I moved in with my cousin for about a month. I had lived in Hawaii for 2.5 years. I rode my bike a lot in Hawaii (that was from the ages of 7-9). I purposefully did not come home all the time. It was when Larry was grooming me and he was on me when I got home from school. He had been in my life for a year and a half, since I was about 5. He hadn't got a good grip on us yet. I would be on my bike all day long avoiding him, until my mother got home. And I would steal food, candy, at the store. I'd go in, get my candy, and then leave. Then I'd ride up to where my mother worked at a Hamburger Joint in Waikiki, and visit her. I remember just feeling so bad so strange. I didn't want to go home and I was scared. Larry would be on me all of the time. This was in the stage where I still had the control. I could say, "No – I don't want you to do that. Don't do that. Stop." But as time went on, it got so that he was more and more controlling over my day to day moves. Then he got really violent, beating my mom up. He was not able to hold a job.

In 1975, I moved in with my Mother's cousin and his boyfriend, who were gay. They were two men who were very loving and nice to me. They taught me trust and colors. They had a lot of music albums – 100's of them. They were classy. My sister was there, too.

One day, I decided to walk to the store by myself. I'm in Huntington Beach, and I walk to the store from the apartments. I grabbed a plastic bag and I stole a bunch of candy, the kind that you weigh. The candy was in bulk at a child's eye level. So, I robbed 4 or 5 pounds worth of candy. Then I walked back home to the apartments and I sold it to all of the kids in the neighborhood. That was so much friggin' fun. I remember thinking that I was a bad-ass because I could sell. Little did I know that the store manager had followed me home and told on me. I didn't get in trouble.

Later, when I was 13, I would walk to the store with food stamps to get all of the groceries for the house. My mother would leave me the money or the food stamps. I would walk alone and make my own decisions – to the same grocery store that I stole in. I learned to steal really young – I was like a kleptomaniac at the age of 9.

I raised my babies with a lot of love. I have a high tolerance for a lot of noise and chaos. I can handle a lot of chaos at once. That's why I was a good caterer.

Larry, when we were getting ready for the new baby to be born, I was in 5th grade. That was a really hard year. Larry was becoming extremely demanding; he didn't just want my body; he also wanted me to commit to marrying him when I turned 18. Out of 24 hours a day, there were maybe four hours total a day that went by without him after me. He'd come into my room in the middle of the night every night. You don't know when you're going to get woken up. So you start to live on a really nervous note. You start to notice everything. As anybody knows when told you can't have something, you want it more. So, my point is that when you're told you can't have certain foods you want them even more. Especially in 5th grade, it seams to be where his turning point was beginning to be very jealous and possessive over me. He would tell me things like "I want to marry you when you turn 18" or "I don't want your mom, I want you." Or he'd say that I was the only one that he really wants; he just touches my sister so she doesn't feel left out.

At the same time, the baby was about to come. At this point, my mother already knew that Larry was a molester. She had a baby with him anyway. Larry said to me one day on the bed in his room, laying there naked, by the way, "Do you think that I should do these things with the new baby girl?" I thought you don't know who you're fucking with. When he said that to me, it shocked me and hurt me. I was scared for the baby. It was a lot of pressure for me. Now I had my sister, my mom, and the baby to look after.

These are some of the traits that these pedophiles do.

After I told on him again, in fifth grade, he came into my room at about 3 AM. He slapped me hard across the face to wake me up. He said that if I ever told on him again, he was going to kill me and my whole family.

There are these quotes on Facebook about not looking back. Why study history, if we don't want to look back? It can show us what we

need to learn sometimes.

I started going to church for the first time in fifth grade. I would pray, and I would have an overwhelming feeling that someone was coming to save me. I had a feeling like help was coming soon.

I had to give him blow jobs; I had to make sure that Larry was taken care of before the bus came. He had to be in a good mood; that means that he ejaculated. Then I could go to church.

In fourth grade, one of the things that Larry liked to do was have my sister and I naked. Whoever lost the game had to give a blow job or have their vagina licked. My mother was very busy then. There was no way she was coming home. Larry would have me and my sister pose like porn stars, and have us lick each other; perform oral sex on each other.

My grandmother (my mom's mom) called Child Protective Services (CPS) once. I thought, oh my God, someone is going to save me. Because I was already trapped by Larry, against my will. They came to the door and Larry said that he was babysitting us, and they went away. My grandma told me, 20 years later, that she had called CPS. My mother had told her mom to stay out of her business.

Back in 1973, one of the grooming things that Larry did was to take showers with me, my mother, and my sister. We moved onto a property that had a banana field in back. There was a gigantic hippy shower that could fit 12 to 15 people in it if you crammed them. You could have a good orgy going on there. My mom, I, my sister, and Larry all took showers together. My mom didn't think anything of it because she didn't have any sexual perversion in her. She should have wondered why I was wearing wet diapers at bed time all of the time. Kids pee when they are distressed. There are signs that you should be aware of.

The Golden Pearl Army

I didn't think of the Golden Pearl Army until 5 or 6 years ago. At the time, I was Mormon, but I don't want to be Mormon again, or any other religion.

It came to me that I was from the Golden Pearl Army.

I was leaving Odessa, TX and I had just had a big estate sale, and I sold such good stuff for cheap. I felt like giving it all away. I had wicker furniture, etc.; we made 900 dollars on everything. We got in the car to come home from Odessa and we were driving, and it was about 4 in the morning. I was really tired. I was feeling so much gratefulness and joy to be moving back because my work was done in Odessa for which I was called there. I was driving at 4 a.m. all alone; my husband had the kids with him in the other vehicle. As I was returning to California, I was saying, "Father, am I pleasing to you?" We were driving down the freeway, and out of nothing, a lady starts descending in lavender with flat gold bells in her hair; with gold trimming around her lavender dress. After her, down came a man in solid bright white. Something was coming to me in solid white. I got so scared, and said, "Not now, not now," and it went away. I was alone. I don't know who the man was but it was the whitest light you could ever sea. I was like, "Oh my God, what just happened to me?"

51

We got to San Diego and I met this girl who worked for my husband. I walked in her bedroom and she had a big lavender candle glowing. I thought it might be a message that the lavender lady was sending me to her. Ever since then, the color lavender has come to me in regards to things that need my attention. I wish that people could have the experience that I had with the lavender lady.

My parents never believed in God, but I already knew him. I knew of a higher God within me. I believed that we were all God's creatures.

The Golden Layered Onion: The Bittersweet Pain of Post-Traumatic Stress Disorder
The Journal of a Child Sex Slave
May 31, 2016

I have no public assistance. No help from the public, so I have to be responsible for myself.

I can live holistically if needed. They are always trying to put me in categories.

They don't understand what it is to be broken.

This is how I can function; you like it, or you don't.

This is what I've been dealing with. I got my GED, and was on Adderall to do it. I no longer take any medication to finish tasks. I do have the loving support of my husband and friends.

I had an idea – I started going through the papers that we did, feeling like a used and abused wet noodle. The suffering things with Larry were so exhausting, and really fucked up.

I want you to sea how this works and how this is happening before our eyes. Pedophilia is about to blow up and start changing. We go around it constantly that no one wants to deal with it because it's hidden. Society and karma are on its way. There is some heavy karma flowing in the winds in Oregon, and it's a domino effect, and they're busted.

I'm excited that I have the energy to release a tear drop resulting in a wave into the universe.

It is men and women together; it's not just men or women, it's both.

How did Martin Luther King, Jr. feel when he was little? He must have had the energy from the get-go. He had a similar passion to Christ's. When you come to the earth and you have a passion, whether you learn it through pain, there is nothing you can do but pursue it. There may be pain. He wanted to protect his people, and I want to protect my people – especially children. There are more problems, and I expect to be a vessel to do that. The point is that I have a passion like Martin Luther King, Jr.'s, that I am not able to control. That is why I have been writing my book on my day-to-day grind since I was the age of four and a half of being trapped, controlled, and brain-washed.

Pedophiles have a gene for it. I haven't met one yet – and I would love to – that can control their pedophilia. It will eat them alive; there is no cure for pedophilia. They are here to destroy the human race, to make man and woman against each other. Using little bodies as sexual objects is a dysfunction that the world cannot ignore.

Once in a while, I will have a prompting to want to spread the word of how pedophilia hurts the world. I want to protest it. I find myself when I'm out in the public, like a popular coffee shop, I will tell one or two people if I have the opportunity to be aware and to protect children at all costs. Meanwhile, I feel overwhelmed and exhausted. What I mean by this is that I don't go many places right now, and when I go into these places, I have an overwhelming feeling come over me that I need to share with the world to protect children. It has been happening to me for a while. It is very hard on me, I'm sure.

I have been broken, and I have used the drugs to dull me. I sometimes have wanted to just be put to sleep for a little while, in a place for my brain to relax. Now, I have no other devices other than to accept who I am and to love myself. I have meditations.

The point of all of this, is that I had a topic that I wanted to get out.

When Child Protective Services (CPS) came to the door, when I was a child in California, nothing happened. When they came to the door, I promise you this, I was thinking, "Please help me." Why couldn't I scream out, "this fucker is abusing me and making me suck his dick!" I couldn't do it because you're a slave. There is the chance that you won't get help and there will be consequences. The consequences are much more likely to happen than anyone helping your ass. That's for fucking sure. They are supposed to protect kids, but they haven't been abused. If you haven't been abused, it's really difficult to walk in those shoes.

Broken angel wing that I have. My left wing (I call it my "wing" not my arm) is broken really. I have to baby it. It's been completely crushed. My boss let me move into his house when I told him about the barrels. Another angel with wings told me that she felt like her wings had been clipped.

I think about it, and I ask myself if I make it up that I'm from the Golden Pearl Army, but then I go long ago – that I could tell what a pedophile was at the age of four and a half without being told. That's when I knew that the Golden Pearl Army is real. This is not about religion. Maybe I was so scared that I had nothing else to hang on to; no, that isn't it. Because no one would help me? No. If your own mother isn't going to help you, who the hell else is? There is an army for the children of God, and it is the Golden Pearl Army. Those are all of the reasons for the Golden Pearl Army.

My sister was two and a half years younger than me. So, I'm the one who protected her. She had her big sister to stand up for her in school, because I could beat up anybody who'd mess with her.

60% of sex abusers have never been sexually abused; 40% are acting out what they went through.

The monster used to tell me stories; he was not abused sexually.

I'm talking about pedophilia – it's a disease.

If you're a pedophile, you can be in the Church and be around children.

They told me that my kids didn't have a real, true testimony of Jesus Christ.

The two categories that I work on to protect humans are:
- Death; and
- Child porn or pedophilia

There's not this many people that have caught all of these pedophiles. I want to talk to people and give them some valuable insight. I can bring a lot of pain to people too, because people want to shush it up.

The Golden Pearl Army – every two or three days, I'm aware of it. I know it – there's too much evidence. It's an awareness like no other. I should have a PhD in pedophilia – I have lived around it for so long as a child.

Pedophiles give a damn buttons are broken. What I mean by this is that pedophiles can molest a child and live with their remorse easily. Their remorse is part of the feeling of control that they have, and the feeling that they might lose it all at the same time – the adrenaline rush.

When I originally moved to Hawaii, it was Larry and my mom; and my dad and his girlfriend, and several other hippies.

I have two sides to me: one that knows expensive taste; and then that side that has been in severe poverty, especially of safety and freedom; poverty of sexual rights; and poverty of people (like my mother) of supervision and safety. Those poverties added up and led me to the Golden Pearl Army.

Now it's harder to balance it. It's like realizing you are "I dream of Jeanie." It's like you have certain gifts that are in one area. It goes back to human rights and children.

I'm embarrassed about having secret love affairs in my heart for other men. I don't know if I'm well enough to be in a super long-term relationship. My husband has set up a lot of problems for me for a lot of the time. A share-load of addictions.

I was warned by my therapist that I would have severe PTSD long before I ever got married.

I think that's when I knew when I caught the 10th most wanted man – that something extraordinary was happening – something special. I could feel it the way it happened. It was obvious that I was there for a reason. As an individual, it is like first time actual validation.

Regarding the messages: all of a sudden you get little messages that the universe is pleased with you. There are souls that have cried out for help, and the Golden Pearl Army sends its messengers (like me) out to help.

When the young boy that I helped, told me that he had been praying for help; I knew that I was there, and I was almost like a version of Mary Poppins' character from Disneyland. It has been an extraordinary journey to leave memories with little children that there are people who care and stand up for their rights.

I have moved my family so much – because I was being called to certain places. Now I'm struggling because I'm no longer being called. (You never know who you're with.) I had a strawberry flower pot, and the plant dropped in its ceramic vase. Now it's rooted in the ground. I felt like that was a message to me to plant myself here, rather than getting a calling and go.

I can so identify with whoever is calling me for help. My sister would cry to me, and I would take care of it. My mother would cry, and I would take care of it. When my mother and Larry had their only child together, I took care of it.

The Golden Layered Onion:
The Bittersweet Pain of Post-Traumatic Stress Disorder
The Journal of a Child Sex Slave
June 7, 2016

I don't know where this is going, but I went to sea The Night of the Living Dead when I was a kid. When the original of that movie first came out, I can still feel pain from a memory - to the point where I can't release it. I know it's not real, and I'm letting it go and all. It's post-traumatic. I can feel that pain right now. I always go to that it could always have been even worse.

In 1972 or 1973, when I saw that film, it came out in the movie theater in Hawaii. I was seven. We had only been in Hawaii about 3 months. I was in a scary theater with several of my mom and dad's hippy friends, who were the ages of 20 – 23 years old. There had been a fire in it and you could smell the fire still. I don't know where my mom was. It was a burnt-down theater. I slept on a floor in a room of grown-ups, and I slept next to Larry's older brother, who was my dad's best friend. He tried to molest me; but in the end he just talked dirty to me. He had the same gene that Larry had. I don't know whether it was the abuse their mother gave them; Larry would always tell me that his mother used to flush his head down the toilet for looking at his sister naked. I think that it's a gene. Because I was horribly abused, and I can't imagine doing that to someone. That's the best that I can tell you.

I did sea the movie The Night of the Living Dead, the end of the night. Larry's brother, Jack, talked sexually to me and held me inappropriately, I was seven and he would have been around 22. There were hot hippy chicks all over the place; so, pick one of them – why pick me, m-fucker? And he was my daddy's best friend, too.

I was there and stuck in it, and dealing with all of these different personalities. I was so aware at the time.

The movie is so scary. What you sea are zombies eating people. It was the original. It was in an old cemetery; the zombies are coming. Larry's brother, Jack, let me down that night. I remember feeling, "Really? Wow, man – another one?" Jack is nice; but as soon as he had the opportunity, he tried something.

Larry spied on me. He started spying on me as soon as he started living with us. It would kick my ass. I'm the best detective ever now. He would be spying on me when I was in the bathroom through the window in the bathroom, watching me shower. I would know it and I would have to deal with it. So much violating and I got so sick and tired of it. It wasn't once a week, it was every day and all day.

Today, that's why I have a nervous system disorder. After I caught Mr. Monster, he sent me over the edge. Once I figured it out, it was like a sick puzzle. It is out of control and you have to accept the truth and it can be very painful. But at the same time, once you know, you don't want to have anything to do with that person, you know that much.

I can be watched and act any way that I need to survive. Because I'm on my toes, and I'm never off of them. It's like I'm twisted; and when you untwist it, you should have left it twisted. That's probably why I have a gift regarding knowledge of pedophilia, and I can pick up on people and their fetishes. Because of Larry constantly watching me all day long, sexually after me, my nervous system seas everything like a photographic memory constantly moving in slow motion and able to take in everything around you. You master your environment without anybody even having a clue, ready or not, whether you like it or not.

I went to Drug and Alcohol School, and they'd all tell me that I was the best interrogator. They started bringing in suicidal people. I had a strong feeling of being afraid of suicide; I was afraid that I couldn't help those people. I remember crying my eyes out as my teacher did a course on suicide. We had to watch a film of people jumping off of bridges. I felt that I had a calling to help suicidal people, but did I have a calling to save them all? No, there is no way that I can. Suicide comes in many forms. I have helped teenagers who have been slowly wanting to commit suicide through their health issues and not even realizing it because they are wretchedly depressed.

One day, I was volunteering in the cafeteria of my son and daughter's elementary school. I met a man who was also a volunteer, and he was mentally challenged. He told me that when he was a little boy he was kidnapped by a pedophile, and he got away. There was a big man who was a janitor; he was probably about

37, and he was very mean. He was tattooed from head to toe and always had a mean grin on his face. The tattoos weren't the scary part; it was the wretched expression on his face that scared me the most. He would give away ticket coupons to kids who would throw their plates in the trash and help clean up. But if you looked at the ticket coupons, they were all expired, meaning that the kids couldn't use them. The kids would have to go with him to get the tickets. This was going on with several little kids. Most of the kids that he was luring seamed to be a bit chunky. He lured them with food and tickets; taking them to the back alone while the teachers were on lunch break. I reported it to the principal because he was taking them to the back alone, and the boy was skipping ahead of him. It is a big deal because no adult should be taking kids somewhere alone. The man that was mentally challenged was there, helping and doing all kinds of work. I was touched by an angel when I met him. I was so glad to report the janitor. I don't know if they did anything about it or not, but I said to the principal that I was sure that the kids' parents would like to know that the janitor is taking these kids alone and giving them invalid tickets. I could feel the misery and wretched pain of both the child and the pedophile, and the disgusting get-after-it disposition that the pedophile had towards these children individually.

I get cases for the Golden Pearl Army, but I truly never want to stop protecting kids. I say after every case that I am done, and I am not going to do this anymore. I pray to God that I am done and have done my duties, but I truly never want to stop protecting kids of their human rights.

I'm not going to be able to stop pedophilia, but I'd like to put a drop in it and splash it to save billions of children, reaching their hands out and screaming and begging for help within themselves.

To go into the Golden Pearl Army

I had another girl asking my kids if they wanted to try heroin. I had to get the kid out of meth houses, etc. After that, I was done with these kids.

It took me to another level. My nervous system is shot. Alcohol can't fix it; I hate pills. They won't give me medicine. I have more problems getting meds than anyone else in my life. It must be because the universe doesn't want me to be on them. BANG!

I decided that I was going to help this church lady. She was 30 years old. (This is Sister Angel.) She was my first person who asked me to take care of her as an adult. She had chronic horrific depression. She had lost five babies – still births. I started figuring out some traits about her and I figured out she was a drug addict – she was on pain killers. I started through DHS's Department for Disabilities to work for her. So, I got certified to work for her. She knew the lady that was sexually assaulting kids at the church. She would tell me in confidence that this woman had gotten in trouble before and the church did nothing about it. She was really sick, but I finally got her to walk. I was helping her, and she'd tell me that she wished I was her mother. I told her that she needed to get off of the pills. One day, we went to the Emergency Room to get her pills. She was really bad off. I told her in the ER Room, I have been doing this for 12 years (for others) and I'm not doing it anymore. She said, "You're quitting?" I said, "I am," and I walked out of the hospital. This was Sister Angel. I had the feeling, and this was like 7 months later, I had that feeling, and she died. I fought with her for months trying to help her out.

I always told myself that I don't want to work with suicide. It makes me very uncomfortable. I have experienced 2 suicide attempts by others that I loved. If I had stayed with her, she wouldn't have killed herself, but I don't take the blame for it because she decided on her own to commit suicide. It was a slow suicide. That sounds very blunt and cold, but you run out of avenues, and sometimes you are not always going to be there on time.

I had a feeling that I never wanted to work with suicides or quadriplegics. I'm working for a quadriplegic now. I have helped many people who have suicidal tendencies to want to live another day.

I was just getting certified and I got a call from the Drug and Alcohol School at Inter-coast College. I went on-line, and she calls me up, and says, "I'm your technical person." She said that her friend was a foster person and she is writing a story on her experience. At the same time, my teacher told me if there's anything I should be doing, it's writing. He said that I have a very dramatic flair.

The Golden Layered Onion: The Bittersweet Pain of Post-Trau-matic Stress Disorder
The Journal of a Child Sex Slave
June 14, 2016

In working my way out of a depression, I find that writing on a little pad of paper, "I love you, Cidney" helps. I do that a lot. The more that I do it, the more that I write, it relieves some pressure. Usually, I put, I love myself very much. Stuff like that. Most people don't have to do that, but it grounds me.

Out of nowhere, Mental Health got me in the same day. I saw the psychiatrist, and he put a psychotic label on me. When I told my boss this this morning, he said that maybe you're having a premonition. Possibly, something is coming - a vision or something. When he said that to me, it did ground me.

To live and to survive, I have to put myself in my own world. I've lived there a long time. But it's real. And I haven't met anyone, or a group yet, that has the same gift that I have yet. When I do, I am excited to meet my fellow man/woman/human that has the same gift as I do. I'd be happy to meet someone who has a similar metronome within themselves.

With my career right now taking care of another man – I was already kind of sick when I moved in there – I got real depressed. Deep depression of the knowledge that men like young girls. The disappointment of that illness, could it be like an alien being taking over the planet?

Why? I want the world to know, and I don't know how else to get to them. So, I have a new idea for us. I was thinking about this: instead of the book being titled The Layered Onion, The Golden Pearl Army is a wonderful name because it is real.

There is an Octopus with a gold chain on her. This particular octopus had been chained up before. I don't know where the story goes. It could be for adults and children. The children are who we need to talk to – whether it's through books. Let them know that they can tell on their parents. But guess what?! You may not get any fucking help! That's where I stop, and put the brakes on. Where am I going with this?

The Golden Pearl Army came to me when I was in Redlands,

CA. It was about five years ago now. A shield of golden armor – in my head. The other part is an octopus lady who has an overloaded sensory system. She picks up on energies. I would describe myself as that. An octopus, when you are coming at it, it will be scared at first until it knows you. It could scatter away. Then it goes into your sensories and tells you all the things that could be wrong. Your brain calculates it through your nervous system. At first, the octopus will scan it with all of its scanners. It has 8 arms. If one gets disappointment, it's got another one. It has so many legs to get done what it needs to do. Until it gets clearer, maybe it'll have thoughts that could be possibilities. After that, there's the proof. There's the BAM – there's proof. No longer afraid. But that's when you get hurt. Because one of the thoughts that you had that wasn't good happened. Your mechanism – your sensor tried to tell you – it's like getting chills down your body from God. That's why there are mechanisms to spread out, or so to speak, veins or tree roots.

God called me to the Center, and to Odessa, and to several other places.

Here's the bad part: if you don't sea any evidence, but you know, you can't prove it.

The rights of humans that are born to the body of earth: their right is to not be hurt. You aren't supposed to hurt newborn babies and children. It's the human right at birth. Everybody needs to take a deep breath and stop and think about that. One of the rights is to protect children from pedophilia. It's a disease and it creates very sad people (some of who have been abused). Within those sad people, there are also very creative, gifted people. Just like everybody else is, it does something to your nervous system. Which will put you in the octopus family. You will no longer be a human, you will be an octopus. The big necklace / chain on the octopus. Picture there's a thick necklace around the octopus' neck.

The Golden Pearl Army

The God of Pain that gives you extra-sensory powers because the ones you were given are being damaged. Your nervous system has to endure days of pain. The Octopus God comes and gives you relief.

I have heard that even the Hawaiians have creation myths that the Octopus is an extra-terrestrial being that came from an earlier universe.

Since I was a very little girl, I loved to talk. My mom asked me why. From the age of 5, I was trapped. At that time you have a feeling of hell, and you can't get out. Every day. I hope that everyone will read this book and will know that, and will be able to stand up when they know. Save a child. Go straight to the rights that the children were born with by law. My mom used to tell me, "Why do you have to talk to everybody?" Then she'd say, "What planet are you from?" I have received acknowledgment from God. He has come to me, and I will not deny him. He does bring me out, but he waits. I'm afraid because I know his power, and what he's capable of. Yes, I have the fear of God, but not the way religion is taught. I have been in churches where they hide pedophiles and even protect them.

I promise you if you could look at a building that never ends, don't think that there aren't well trained army sent here to do this work. All that I can think is that I am the most sophisticated business woman working for the Golden Pearl Army. When I get in the hunt mode, that's when I become the octopus.

When I wrap all eight of my arms around them, and take them down. Through scary corners they never knew they could find an octopus leg. God puts me right there. It's like I'm driving a fancy car, and I'm on a business trip.

Part of the business trip is that I'm on a mission for real, and I go under cover, and I go into different personalities. People want to call me crazy, but it's not – I know why I'm here. Do you?

I want everyone to know that I have been so molested, but thank God, I can still enjoy sex. I don't care who you are – you can still have a healthy life.

I can pick up on sexual dysfunction, bull shit, and those who lie, good.

So, when these doctors are diagnosing me with this stuff, I find it ironic that I'm telling them about children being abused in their community, and instead of saying, "let's go and take care of the kids," they want to assign a label to me – psychotic or manic or whatever. That's bullshit.

I'm grateful that psychiatrists are here, but we need to be thinking a bit higher up and look down at the whole room.

If we have to climb a fucking ladder and look at the picture, and sea the whole picture, not just one thing in the picture.

It's like a snail effect – you think you're going to get help, and then, wham they got you again.

The Golden Layered Onion:
The Bittersweet Pain of Post-Traumatic Stress Disorder
The Journal of a Child Sex Slave
June 21, 2016

Being molested, for a long time, you don't have boundaries or set them for others. So, I can easily get bullied. I don't bully, but I can get bullied. I'm not the perfect little angel, but my boundaries from being molested for so long - I can go along with what others would consider unacceptable behavior.

It happens to me (getting bullied) all of the time. I was just helping Nan (when the counselor said we were "inappropriate" for the group session).

[Nov. 5th - Nan and I share a birthday (but different birth years).]

Regarding my boss, I don't want to tempt him if giving him a hug is inappropriate. He let it go too far, going up my shorts every time. My boss agreed that he wouldn't do that anymore, although he still wants the hugs. He doesn't have anyone touch him ever.

Until I got this raise, I didn't have a lot of money. Even though I have helpers, I pay them myself.

Since I have no boundaries, I can get violated.

I've been doing the meditations. I wake up much better from that.

One of the things that I am really screwed up with is underwear. Larry would grab my underwear and smell them and keep them. I'm always worried that someone is going to get me or my daughters' underwear. I worry really badly. I'm unwell over it. But I've been doing meditation to try to get over those thoughts because Larry doesn't live with me anymore. He doesn't haunt my mornings, afternoons, and evenings.

So, that's where I'm at every day.

The wretchedness of it is that I fear for children all the time. But since listening to the meditations, I've been able to actually watch TV programs and like them. But the train still goes off the track and crashes, one day good and one day bad. One hour good, the next hour crying.

Can't find myself. I lost sense of myself, almost like going into a coma – a trance type coma.

My sister had me all day long, and I was very much of a protector. I was like a soldier girl. I remember if anyone messed with my sister, it stabbed me.

She broke down and I would say that I'd do it, and I'd take care of it. She still had to do it, but not as much as me. Larry would tell me that he really only wanted me.

Larry would go in and out of adult to child in talking and voice and body gestures. He would act really young, like an eight year old. Right around the time he was abused by his mother. He would regress into childhood with irrational behavior. At 8, you become more conscious of yourself, and that's where he was stuck. He'd go in and out of it, and go into raging tantrums. He'd dump all of my clothes on the ground and all the clothes off of their hangers and then make me rehang them. He'd punish us in his tantrums. He was also very abusive to the dog. He would sit in silence, and he would get mad at himself for what he wanted to do to us. And his anger would build up and he'd take it out on me.

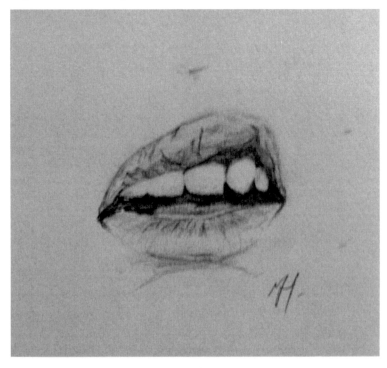

The Golden Layered Onion:
The Bittersweet Pain of Post-Traumatic Stress Disorder
The Journal of a Child Sex Slave
June 29, 2016

Got up gently out of nothing. My nervous system could feel it from far away. I have an over-developed nervous system from living with a pedophile who abused me. If you come to the reality of it, it could be completely overwhelming.

Got a feeling in my brain this morning. It's like a vibration and I have had it for years and I could go into it twice this morning. From the age of 14, I've had it. It used to be loud or louder, and then it subsided. It would come and go depending on how still I get. I haven't had it in a while. But from the age of 14, I've had it off and on. It's some sort of nerves thing from living with someone who has this disease. Your nervous system is shattered – from trauma or terror.

Even though it's a terror that can be a day to day grind. That's why I am so concerned for others because I know what it does to them. I want to help people become aware of it so that they don't have their fellow man being abused by this sick disease for which we have no cure. I think it's an alien – it's not 100% human. That's my opinion.

Life of surviving someone who has this disease.

I'm talking about the ones who have died from it. There was a little girl who was 4, and I was 40, when she died. She was found dead in the bushes not far (maybe 10 miles) from my home. She was raped and killed.

There are some people out there that just can't imagine what it's like and they feel for the pedophile. Those are the ones that are prevailing and allowing this to continue. They better get a backbone fast. Their karma will come back to get them. I am the messenger to say this to the world.

Your duty as a human being.

My sister isn't like this but then I was taking care of her. She always had me there. We are not from the same planet. We are sisters on this planet and she was blessed to be with me. And yes, she feels that. She would lay her life down for me. But she is weak; I had to protect her or she could have melted quite quickly to another dimension in her mind that wouldn't let her be where she is today.

It is like the Cinderella show. My mother was so jealous that she prevented me from being with my father.

In home fronts that have sexual dysfunction there can be a lot of jealousy.

Once you know that someone is hurting a child; you know. You don't go to bed that night, and say I'll deal with it later, I'm going to forgive him. Don't believe it won't happen again. They'll keep doing it or they'll kill themselves. So you can't live with it another day. The person who is enduring it is not the person who needs to tell. You can picture a thick ice lake, and your child under that ice. You need to get that pick and hammer your baby out of that ice.

This particular alien disease, it's not like transvestitism – it's not at all in the same category. This goes to where the person doing it is stuck at the age where something bad happened to them. 60% of pedophiles have never been molested; 40% have. I don't care what happened to them; if they don't have the gene, they won't be a pedophile. There has to be a dysfunction in the "Give a Damn" button.

Music saved my life and soul.

Larry played guitar and I played the tambourine, and I'd sing, and we had a band. He played house with us; cowboys and Indians; pornography. Foods rubbed on his dick. Telling me that foods were made from dicks. Obsessive-Compulsive disorder. This is not a full-blooded human. Maybe there's some kind of wolf-animal in them.

It wasn't until more recently that young children were protected from these beasts.

The Golden Pearl Army wants there to be no more mistaken information on when to get help. Just follow directions and your children can get better. If you don't, your child can have horrible repercussions later, and so will the family.

It's really that bad. It's called torturous dungeon. It happens all over the place.

Take the steps to protect our human race. Don't put it into other colors. Put it into the human race.

I don't like abuse. For those survivors, who have gone through this and feel uncomfortable around intimacy, you have to fake it until you make it. You can have a good fantasy, like you really love that house, or would like a family, etcetera. For survivors, they go through uncomfortable feelings all of the time. We are going to keep having them, but we can ease them with what is right and what we want in our life. The best your loved ones can do when you are going through the bad days, your loved ones should tell you that they love you. When you get like that, then you just have to keep doing meditation and reprogramming those thoughts which are related to the thoughts you were afflicted with during the sexual abuse.

That's what I've been doing. If you don't have a spouse who is supportive, you may have to lose the spouse. Be honest with your spouse from the beginning and work on reprogramming.

I will ask my husband, 3-5 times a day, are you sure you want to be with me? Are you sure you want to be with me when I'm old? Are you sure you don't want to be with a younger girl? He tells me that I have this thing – that I forget in my whole mechanism that my husband even likes me. A pretty wretched pain. Recently exacerbated by the trauma with the Center and the pedophilia there and in the church.

This is very important to me, so this is how I'm doing it. Please don't tell your children not to be tattle-talers anymore. If they need to tell; they should tell.

I just can't imagine it – these are your people. I want to make sure that people tell if they sea something bad. Tell, if you need to tell something; no more of this "don't tattle-tale" bullshit. Once they do it, they can go buy the button that says, "That was easy." They don't need to raise cowards. That's bullying.

How you love your children is how you're going to keep living.

Even the sickest who have been beaten into cowardice, they can rise above it, be strong and change. We can stand up for the rights. We can start programming our children about this type of stuff.

Octopus

The Octopus lives deep in the dark. They sea well and they feel things all around them, and are still able to do what they need to do in the dark. They hear a buzzing vibration, I think. So, I didn't really notice and understand myself that I like to be in the dark sometimes. I don't sea as well as most. I didn't like for Larry to know where I'm at – I think that's what this is from. Make it a bit harder for Larry to get to me, and he'll trip and my mom will wake up. Or he'll get snapped back out of his obsessive-compulsivity and get some fuckin sense into him to leave me alone. (That will never happen.) In return, all it made was more of a hunt for him.

Cinderella

My mother and my sisters treated me like they never liked me; it started when I was about 7 years old. My mom knew what Larry was capable of and she would leave me at home with the Beast. That to me, is no good. (NO GOOD!) They treated me like I was dumb; like my opinion didn't matter, or left me out of things. They bullied me for most of my life. My sister to this day still tells me that I never finish anything that I start. (Although my sister and I are now close, she did call me crying and apologizing to me out of the blue when I was about 33 years old, telling me how sorry she was for how she and my mother and my other sister treated me badly for all of those years. I was grateful to hear that and I know how hard it can be to fall in a trap, to join a group, to bully. All my life I had to take care of bullies, Larry was a bully; all of the kids that used to be mean to my sister, and my mother.) From the age of 13, when my real father called up and told my mom to report it or I'll take my daughters away from you, then Larry was sentenced for the first time. That's when my mother and I became at war. She was mad that my father Bill came through; even though he was a drug addict. But I was so happy; it was the best day of my life. It was like having chains lifted off of me. Someone saved me, and it happened to be my real daddy. I was so happy.

I was really good looking and had all of the guys. My mom had problems with jealousy because of her men wanting me. Every man my mother ever dated hit on me. One asked me to go jaccuzying with me, and I was only 13 years old. One of the men came to my bedroom door with a bare back and no clothes on, just a towel wrapped around him, and wanted me to massage him. I know that there are children going through this right now that maybe this book will get to.

Larry's first sentence was for 2-3 years in a mental hospital and then 2 years in jail.

We children will forgive our parents for so much. Just like they say that God will forgive you. I hate to break it to the world, but God doesn't forgive pedophiles because they can't get any better. Deep in their hearts, they don't, they can't, and they won't get better.

The Golden Layered Onion: The Bittersweet Pain of Post-Traumatic Stress Disorder
The Journal of a Child Sex Slave
July 5, 2016

When I was 20 years old, I got a book called You Can Heal Yourself, by Louise O'Hay. I recommend it. It's a thin book. She's a really nice lady. I studied her book for years. Did meditations; self-affirmations, etc. When I was that age, those helped a lot. Around the age of 28, I stopped using them. Now, I have gone back to using them. The book talks about disease in the body, and how we create our own problems. Lower back pain can mean money problems. As you get older – it's real! Without the meditating and the writing, I'd be lost right now. I didn't even know at the age of twenty that I could read. I had no awareness at all.

<u>Rape</u>

When I was 15, I lived in El Toro, California, and me and my good friend wanted to get to the Cuckoo's Nest, which was a punk-rock night club place where I worked. Black Flag; the Adolescents, and all those bands from those days were playing there. I had cut all my hair off and was doing LSD. (I went through a month and a half, or 2 months, doing LSD.)

One day, we were desperate to get there, and it's a 45-minute drive. My friend was 18 and I was 15, and these two Marines picked us up. We hitch-hiked. They were in uniform at the El Toro base. They held us up with a knife, and passed the freeway. They said as long as we did what they wanted, they wouldn't kill us. They took us to orange groves. One house was there in thirty to forty acres. We went way deep into the orange grove. I got so scared at first. I was terrified that they'd kill me. They said that as long as we do what they want, they would set us free. The black guy started French kissing me, and the white guy had sex with me, and I had to give him a blow job. The black guy raped my girlfriend at knife point while I was with the other guy.

We both handled it very differently; she cried and screamed, and I negotiated. When they found out that I was only fifteen they kicked us out of the car with no clothes on. So, we're in the middle of the orange grove, and we're naked. It's probably about 9

72

PM at this point. All of a sudden we saw them coming back. We were scared. But they threw our clothes out of the car and took off. These guys were in their thirties. They left us again. My friend was hysterical. I was saying we needed to get it together. The people at the house took us to the emergency room.

A few months later, we saw them and got their license plate. We went to court and we lost. Their wives were both pregnant in court. My friend told me, don't say we were hitch-hiking because her mom would be mad at her. We got in voluntarily, by hitch-hiking, so we lost in court. But they really did rape us. They got away with it - this is in Costa Mesa, California. I never hitch-hiked again.

Another Rape

I was 18, and I had made friends with a cop. I was living in Mission Viejo. One night, my house was unlocked, and he knew where I lived. We were acquaintances from him pulling me over one time. He'd never been in my room before. He came in to my house uninvited while my mother was there asleep. He put his penis in my mouth; he came all over me and then left. I couldn't believe it was happening to me! Pretty violating to be raped in your own home. That was the last time I ever saw him.

So, that happened to me.

When I was 14, because I was in 7th grade, and I got held back one year, I made a friend in class. He was a lonely boy, and nobody liked him. He used to hitch-hike a lot. He smoked pot. One day, I gave him a bag. I would go out of my way to say "Hi" to him. One day in Huntington Beach, this was about 37-38 years ago, he was hitch-hiking and he got picked up by the Freeway Killer. He was murdered by him; he cut him up into pieces and left him by the highway. The Freeway Killer is horrific. We all had to go to his funeral. One day, when I was 38 years old, I was driving down the road and all of a sudden someone comes on the radio and this man gets on by phone, and said that he was driving down Beach Blvd., and saw a man in a black van, and felt the fear of the devil go through him. The next day, they said that they found the Freeway Killer in the black van.

Then, when I was 45 or 46, I decided to look up the Freeway Killer's sentence. The day that I did that was the exact same day that he was being sentenced to death that night. That guy brutalized this young boy. That was a very hard experience to go through. That was a weird experience.

I want to talk about forgiveness. I don't know where to begin with it. It's like being in a box and you're a rat and there's no way out but to forgive. If you forgive it, you can move on. This is in reference to my mother mainly, who I adore, and who has hurt me terribly without knowing it. I broke down and I went back to her. I had stopped being around my mother because of children's rights. How am I standing up for children if I don't stand up for those rights? I have lost friends for being a tattle-tale.

Some people might say, "You bitch, you're ruining families." That was how it was in the church; I was getting looks that were just terrible. I reported the lady from the church and she got in no trouble at all. And that was from reporting it to the church hierarchy and to the police. I had people in the church tell me, please don't report. I look at them saying, *and her son is being raped?*

As far as the rape is concerned, I was a wild woman for years anyway, drinking, and doing speed, etc. I was doing crank from ages 15 to 18. I got it out of my mother's vial. Us mothers, we do the best we can. She didn't give it to me; I stole it from her. It was called crank. I'd put a pinch in my coffee, and I could go to school and I could function. Otherwise, I had a lot of anxiety.

One day, I decided I was sick and tired of drinking speed, so I threw it down the toilet. By 18, I was done with any drugs. I don't know how I made it. But this is easy-street compared with some kids' stories out there. I want to reach out to those people so that they know that they aren't alone. People have all types of self-help books from people who haven't been raped.

I want to tell them that the only way out is to have people that love you; meditate; and do self-affirmations.

They need to report the abuser to relieve their stress of it. Doing so validates us and gives us power and strength.

One day, I was speaking with a guy who had been molested by his babysitter. I was about 30. He was very over-weight, and the guy that raped him is still out there, molesting. This guy would regress, like most of us survivors – handle things or rationalize them like children. He was trapped in that because he hadn't reported the abuser. I hope that I made a dent in his heart.

74

Forgiveness

I have to forgive myself for a couple of cases of abuse that I didn't report because I had no proof.

I had a lady that I was friends with about 8 years ago. Both her sons were being molested at home by their father, and he'd go on vacation with the boys and leave the mother at home.

The youngest boy, who was 8, he had worms. He would come over to my house and try to talk about it and his brother would shush him. His older brother would run around in girl's clothes. The other boy would look at me, when I'd leave with his mother. "Please take me," the boy would say. I could smell molestation; I could smell it and feel it. I had to sit at the dinner table with the father who was so sick.

The little boy wrote that his daddy liked him to play with his bat.

I can't save them all. I ended up telling my best friend about it, and she was friends with the mother. They had a Big Brother, and he was molesting. He got taken down because he had a record and they hadn't checked him. They really need to check people at children's foundations because that's where the molesters will work. They'll volunteer, easily, to do it; not all, but many.

Forgiveness related to abuse as a child. I don't think that deep down there is any real forgiveness. Maybe we can forgive but we don't forget.

I don't mind forgiving but you don't let it go. You're going down for it. You're busted.

Forgiveness and Resentment

I think about Larry daily – yeah. He goes through my head daily. Like when I'm in the store picking out a cucumber – like I'm picking out a certain sized dick. I feel very uncomfortable. I also worry that my husband could be bad and I don't catch it. I worry that my kids could be hurt, and I can't save them. They tell me nothing is happening.

Like at church, they'll say, who would volunteer to help in the nursery. That's a perfect place for a pedophile.

My daughters were groped by my mother-in-law's husband. She chose to be with him over us. He'd also whip my son with a wet towel. I had a feeling about him; I should have trusted my feelings, and sure enough he got to them. He used to take them alone when they were 3. We have no proof; no DNA. All we have is what my children have told us.

It's been a long journey to stand up for the rights of children. It has been exhausting, but I don't want to give up.

Some groom with love, and some groom with meanness. Some intermix it.

Larry was mixed; he was mean, and also very loving. He was mean if he didn't get what he wanted; and loving if he did get what he wanted.

Secretly, behind his back, he didn't really control me, <u>because I'm a warrior.</u>

There are so many people this is happening to. Maybe if they read this, they'll stop it.

I have the body energy nervous system like an octopus. (I know I'm not an actual octopus.) If I talk like that in the world, they'd say that I'm psychotic. The associations for me - my tools – are the Golden Pearl Army (the Children's Army) and the Octopus.

I've had signs come to me to tell me this through coincidences, symbols, and I put it together myself. The Golden Pearl Army is for children. It's a tool that I'm going to use.

The Golden Pearl Army just like the golden light from Buddha or whoever – it's a belief in a system of radiance of child protection from God. The Golden Pearl Army doesn't have gray. There's no gray there. It's black and white.

I'd love to have a bumper sticker that says, "TheGoldenPearl-Army.com" – I could help children by having people go in under-cover into schools to find molesters. The Golden Pearl Army doesn't believe in "minding its own business" because the children are its business.

The Octopus is from being spied on 24/7. Molesters can barely sleep through the night because all they think about is you, and at all times. Four to five times a day, and then all day spent spying.

This pedophile starts thinking jealousy, anger, manipulation. Once his sexual needs are met, he feels safe and validated and calm again. That's just Larry's type of illness. Something you never imag-ined that could be in your house. Who the fuck brought him here?! How is he living with me?!

Talk about when my sister tried to tell my mother about Larry.

My sister lay down and started humping the ground to show what Larry does to us to show my mom. I was always trying to protect my mother's feelings. That's where I know when there are pedophiles is because I know my behavior.

Sometimes it's not always who we think it is.

The Golden Layered Onion: The Bittersweet Pain of Post-Traumatic Stress Disorder
The Journal of a Child Sex Slave
July 29, 2016

I am re-programming my paradigms. It's a difficult task; I have to tame them all.

I've been listening to a man named Bob Proctor; and I listen to another meditation religiously.

What a pedophile does to the brain is horrific and I fight the battle.

They have a belief when they wake up every day. They have a low tolerance to discussing their age. They don't like getting old. They get really sensitive about that. You'll notice that in them.

They get to the point to where they're a ten year old arguing it. I have sean one time and again. I lived with one for 7 years. I saw it with someone who came after my daughter. I figured out my daughter was at risk, and I got her out.

At the time, I didn't realize how bad some of them are. They will rape and kill.

I had one in my home once who was headed in that direction. In his car, he had about 15-20 stuffed animals, all along the back. He liked 4 to 5 year olds up to 9 years old. Anything after that was too old for him. This one was going to start a book company with my husband and he had all of the signs (including trapping my five year old daughter in the hall). I made the mistake of putting a picture up of my children in my husband's office. That's what happens, <u>they will try to get to know you in order to get at your children.</u>

At a party, out of 10 men or women, one of them separated himself and he was at the slide, watching the little girls go up and down the slide. I showed my friends what he was doing, and they were blown away.

I'm not saying that just because someone holds their daughter, that's sexual. I get triggered because I have post-traumatic stress disorder, so I give the person the benefit of the doubt. Then I catch them.

We could be talking about it, and he wouldn't even hear us.

He came to my house, this is a long time ago, when I had a six year old, and a one and a 2 year old. The man separates – so, at a party, you'll notice that they separate themselves because that's what they're thinking about. He was after my daughter. It was scary. I was not imagining it. Even my daughter remembers it.

[If you watch that show (it's a movie) – it's about a man who got out of prison for pedophilia, and he is trying to fight it. They're dangerous, and it's a wretched sadness for all. Pedophilia kills. It kills the soul; whether you are it doing it, or those who are being harmed. They cannot stop the pedophilia. But I guess there has to be someone in the world who can stand up for the rights of children against pedophilia.]

We have to give children armor against pedophiles. I once heard that women pedophiles are the sneakiest and meanest. I don't believe that, though. I think male or female pedophiles are equally horrific. Would you let a walking dead flesh eater in your house for dinner? Would you let a blood sucking non-restrained vampire to a dinner party?

Mr. Monster was the worst that I ever endured out of all my pedophile catches. He had the entire community tricked. Either that, or half of the community is in on it. It's been going on for so long – over two decades?! I don't know how many children have been at the raft of this monster's side.

One of the mothers thanked me for coming forward.

How many years was he there? A couple of decades! There is sick pedophilia in there that they need to get rid of. Being in the position that I was in, and getting fired was bad news. Worse than that, Mr. Monster tricked me the most. He only got me 3 months and then I busted him. But little Diamond is safe now, and that's what I care about. I have never been so afraid in my life. They fired me because I busted them. It was unbelievable.

There was another monster working there, who all day long would groom one kid, he couldn't think of anything else. He would lay on the grass and roll on it with five to eight year old boys, who would be crawling all over him. He would lay on the ground and groom them to him. These were very lonely boys at home; very vulnerable children with very hard lives. I understand that people wrestle and it is such a hard call to make, but there are other ways to give young boys appropriate manly interactions.

Once I figured this out, I started going into a deep trance.

Mr. Monster fed me bull shit. I played the game with him for about 3 months before I was able to tell that he was a pedophile and that there were a few in there. Did I get to prove it? Yes and no. But Mr. Monster had to resign. He had two offenses with the same girl. It was horrific what they were doing to that family.

I was in a trance (PTSD-trance - almost like a zombie). I live and function, but I go into the function of working for the Golden Pearl Army. Once I know they're a pedophile, I will report it, I will save the child; I will ask the kids if they are safe. They were abusing kids emotionally with food. You would die if you saw their diet. They need nutrition. I was a failure at this. I should have gone off on these two men. Emotionally, I started to go down. I told my husband that he better leave now, because I am going down fast. My brain will no longer be functioning because the Golden Pearl Army is taking over. I'll be on one thing only, trying to get help for these kids, no matter how I have to act.

I was in Redlands when I got the calling to help some kids. While interviewing in Oregon, and meeting the staff, and the whole time, I was a servant for the Golden Pearl Army. I arrived in a cream colored suit. I had not one iota to catch bad guys. I just knew he was sending me to come. The blessings were that they handed me a 6,000 square foot home, and all I had to pay was $500 a month, I had a food allowance, and I was supposed to be paid about $5,000 a month once Mr. Monster approved me for therapeutic foster care, and I was approved for that position. He wrote it all in and sent it in to Mental Health. He made it all up. Under his B.A., I could be a therapeutic foster care parent; but it was made up, because when I called DHS, they said that it's up to him and we don't know why he's doing that. He wanted to be my respite worker, so that he could be in my house overnight so that he could get at my kids. He had 3 foster homes, he would travel from house to house for respite care – in-house pedophilia.

I reported on his offspring as well because of what some children had told me. He was sick and I saw it. He was grooming those boys and I saw him. They investigated and found nothing. It was really sad.

Having them fire me and not following up to protect the children was shattering to me. Children are fragile. They have been hurt bad to the point where we want to stop it, not continue it. Any facility needs to be a calming place, and not an abusive place. How the fuck are the children going to get better if they are still in a hostile environment?

I called two of our foster children after they had got to go home, and asked if they were safe, and they said, "Yes." I said "Good," and then I was out of their lives. I told one of them, "God sent me here from the Golden Pearl Army to protect you." He said to me, I did pray to God for him to save me.

When my husband was out of it due to overdosing on methadone, I said, "Lord, I need a blessing."

At 45, I got my GED; if I wasn't on legal speed, Adderall, I wouldn't have done it at that time. I was dealing with my husband's addiction, etc. He got addicted to opiates after being on them as a child due to an accident. And I was taking Adderall for supposedly being diagnosed with extreme levels of ADHD.

Check out "Law of Attraction" meditation – it's life changing. But you have to go back to it over and over again. Just do it repeatedly, and your subconscious will take it in. Also sea Bob Proctor's meditation: "Six days." They'll help you figure out how to separate what you want to do – to organize it. Thinking of how you should be and act.

The Layered Onion is my childhood.

The Octopus section is how I have caught some of the pedophiles.

The Golden Layered Onion: The Bittersweet Pain of Post-Traumatic Stress Disorder
The Journal of a Child Sex Slave
August 9, 2016

A lot of people stay with pedophiles. The person in the relationship is so insecure and dysfunctional that they are under a spell and can't get out. But they can get out.

I was so fucked up from being molested for so long. Your brain gets so twisted. You don't know who to trust. As you get older, you notice that it becomes more apparent.

I need a lot of reassurance that my husband loves me, and I ask him about this daily.

I have more good characteristics to me that make a man want to be with me anyway.

Doing the affirmations daily makes me feel good every day, and it's not a pill.

Putting them all over the house makes you self-train your paradigms.

There has to be a part of your brain that has not been corrupted that can heal you. If you heal that tiny part it can take over and spread. It only takes one step forward. You'll have more forwards than backwards in the end.

How do your kids handle what's happened? I've raised my kids to be from the Golden Pearl Army, the army for children.

My eldest says, "Mom, if you feel so bad, why don't you go back on your medicine?" Like me, my youngest daughter and son can spot pedophiles.

I want to start the Golden Pearl Army as a foundation for survivors with PTSD.

My father left me, he abandoned me for drugs. He knows that he abandoned me for drugs and other women, and because he couldn't stand to be around my mother.

Because of my mother's vindictive jealousness, she kept me from my father. But he was abusive to her. He was not physically abusive to me or my sister.

All of my kids know that I have a gift of saving children. They may need to mature a bit more for them to really understand it.

The Mormons have a patriarchal blessing. You go to the person that has been blessed to be the person that reads. You go to their house and they put their hands on you; this patriarchal blessing is done by one person in each ward. It's always a man. He told me that all of the children of the church would be looking up to me, and that I am a leader of Zion. Then, that's when I got – two to three years later – I got the calling to come to Oregon to work at the Center. I had the calling to get those kids safe in there, believe me.

Some people may say I'm obsessive / compulsive, but fuck them. When you have been trained in combat you're a whole new person, and I have been trained in combat of child abuse.

How'd I get involved with the Mormons? A friend of my son was Mormon and they invited us to church, and my husband and I went – we were searching for a church, and we liked it there.

We were spiritually searching. Churches are small for me, because I have a higher than a church on earth search. At church you do fellowship and you do affirmations. You're around other people.

I believe the Mormon Church has wonderful values but there are so many humans, we have to be able to accommodate all of them. We all can talk to God, and we all can get messages from God. That's what I believe. They say teach your children about God so that they can pray to him quickly.

I have heard that the Hawaiians think the octopus is a god – no wonder I love them.

You sea a lot of gold with the Egyptians. The Golden Pearl Army is a big deal and it's for the human race.

They can join it and belong to it.

Some people believe in the Salvation Army. They have clothes, and they have drug rehab. They have paperwork on how it should be handled. The Golden Pearl Army believes that everybody that can should wake up today and make sure that children are safe on this planet from sexual harm. In some way or another, we all need to make a change, and we go from here.

I'm so screwed up mentally with feeling loved. It's gotten worse. Maybe the kids kept me busy. Now that the kids are kind of scattering, and going through their own decisions, I worry that he is going to leave me all of the fucking time. I'm worried he is going to go gay on me. I'm not the type to cheat on my husband. I'm not living a lifestyle of being gay. I'm open for others to be that way, as long as they're honest. I worry that he likes other women. It's a constant worry. Sometimes I don't want to be in a relationship because it is so hard for me. I'm telling him, if you want to be with someone else, please tell me. He tries to reassure me over and over. Somehow I can't get it. At times my husband will say, "You're scaring me." Meaning that he is afraid that I might leave him because I think he doesn't love me when he really does. He said that I need a video of him telling me how much he loves me, similar to the movie, 50 First Dates. That's what led me to fear for my relationship, that I needed help, so I started to reframe my paradigms, and I'm allowing the universe to unfold on a day-to-day basis. He does get jealous and doesn't want me to be with another man at all.

The Center

They came over and did a big report. Mr. Monster had to resign as the director, and then they fired me.

I got no whistle blower protection. I can't tell you how much I have been bullied. But what people don't understand about me is that I give God 150% of my trust that he will keep his promises. If there is one person that I can trust – the only person – that will be God from the Golden Pearl Army, the army of children.

I'm sorry to the people that love me and that I love that I don't trust very good. Please forgive me; I am working on it.

When you know you had your spiritual experience. That happens to me but on the evil side; the pedophile's evil side comes out, and I'm after them. Meaning that you close your eyes and when you open them, you are in a battled field. With all due respect to pedophiles who can and do resist, thank you so much for that power and that righteousness. Love, Cyd.

Right when I got Mr. Monster, these evil spirits came for me. I was hoping for a ray of hope. I went to the bus stop and there was this man who was not all there. He was making little noises; almost like a sedated monster. I was in this tunnel and really sensitive to extraordinary beings, both bad and good. Or able to feel vibrations of other humans. This man started talking about an 11 year old girl. He talked about seaing her, but her parents don't want him there. It was like he was feasting. I had to ride with him from

84

one part of Oregon to another. He started making more and more noises, the closer he got to the girl's house. I wrote it all down. Breathing heavy; all of his symptoms. He got off the bus. He was feasting off his desire for this girl.

It was almost like Mr. Monster wanted me to catch him. Some of these pedophiles are so bad off – they don't know how to stop themselves. If you read psychology books, they may not even know when they are doing it.

My stepdad used to cry and say "We can't do this anymore," but he'd go right back to doing it.

Books on my mind:
<u>Chapters</u>
- Hero of the year
- Man comes for dinner
- Larry got in my Volkswagen
- Evidence left in the mind
- Illusions of love
- My pirate
- Hide and go seak
- Booger monster (chaser)
- Hurts animal in yard
- Cowboys and Indians
- Consciousness /awareness (at age 4, saying, "oh fuck" in my head about Larry)
- Scary Monsters
- Drunk Monster
- Dancing for niceness, sexual oral play with sister
- Left with Enimie – don't lie – sorry daddy
- Teacher (Miss Wood) in 5th grade
- Freeway Killer
- Love Story Fades
- Love Strikes
- Heart Reached Truth

List 5 scenes from my life:
- Purple butterflies, big caves, waves, and a long day in the water with my eyes open looking at fish and riding big waves.

Feeling the waves mist on my face; a wind, and cool water.
- Young girl riding her bike in the rain alone. She rides on her own with nowhere to go. She stills to survive and helps the locals survive.
- Right off the plane in Waikiki. Cool evening breeze. "Aloha," the nice man says, giving everyone who gets off the plane a lei. You can smell the flowers in the air, as we got off of the plane. Walking out of the airport, we went to McDonald's – we had yummy burgers there for 0.10¢.
- As I looked around, I could feel the Hawaiian air. I thought to myself, "I love this place." Around me were Hari Krishnas standing all around McDonald's. I thought to myself, I'm going to do what they are doing, so I stood outside McDonald's saying, "Can you spare 0.10¢, please?" I guess you would call that begging. All I know is that my mom and dads were needing help and I was going to come to the rescue. So, there I was at 7 years old, right off of the plane, begging with the Hari Krishnas. Loving my freedom.*
- *"Freedom," my mother says, "That's what she thought that was?" Well, let me tell you what, we just got off the plane; everybody is getting their luggage, and I have two little girls running around, up and down, and all these men dressed in orange blocking my way into McDonald's. They are begging me for 0.10¢, and I'm barely making it here with my husband on another planet, and my boyfriend on a space ship, and I'm looking for my 7 year old and she's out begging for money with the Hari Krishnas.
- Walking to the grocery store for food on a sunny afternoon. She walks, and as she is walking she comes across an extra shopping cart, which she takes back to the store where she shops for her family with food stamps, then travels back home. She has just turned 11, so she can have her own grocery list.

Larry told me that my mom didn't love me or that rather she was mean to me and she didn't love me, but she would leave me alone with Larry for weeks.

Fucked up – 3 sheets to the wind. Always have been crying as I watch my stepdad lie and rape me all day long. "Negro lips" is what he called me, and he always kept his eye on me: in the shower, in the store, in the food market, in the liquor store.

The Golden Layered Onion: The Bittersweet Pain of Post-Traumatic Stress Disorder
The Journal of a Child Sex Slave
September 6, 2016

Example of a way of looking at things. I once came across a young mother who would leave her baby in a car seat, day in and day out. This is just an example of a reality where if a baby is stuck in a position, it will form in that position. I told the mother that you need to lay a blanket down and let the baby sit and lay on the blanket and roll around to use its body. That's healthy. If a plant is put into a bigger pot, the roots expand and it grows. If the plant is left in a tiny pot, it can't expand and it will eventually die. Also, that young mother has to be careful of the people that will come into her life to get at that baby because she is a single parent.

Some say, we all bear a cross. Think about that. My cross if I had one, would be the Golden Pearl Army, that I am here to bring more awareness for other children who are still out there suffering. I believe in the shining planet's star. I believe that the golden light is something that we all are searching and reaching for, and all I sea are children's arms reaching out for someone to save them, who are still actively suffering from pedophilia because they are being molested as we speak and no one can sea it.

The Golden Pearl Army, I believe the government is going to come up with a star planet that has a planet like ours. When we're helping little people, they're our next generation for the planet. We're helping our human planet. That sounds kind of weird, but I am weird, in a good way.

Now, they'll be talking about the golden star planet that has earth-like possibilities. I'm pretty sure that that planet doesn't want to have sickos running it. I'm sorry about that. I just don't want little children to go through what I lived, and to know for all children that they don't like it and it really hurts them. I think you have had to go through it to understand it, and that's why I wanted to help people understand. There are angels, and they are out there searching for closure of what they have gone through. Some are dead and some are alive.

There are 2 sides to this game (like a shuffle board). One side has a round ball and it has a bunch of pokey blades around it, and the master of this side throws the ball in and hopes it can wipe out as much as it can. The other side has buildings up to protect anything that might come in for them to win. The side where the pedophiles live is where the ball is; they hope they can wipe out the human race.

I know about it, because I'm on a conscious different level for the earth. He wired me. My wires got really advanced. I'm trying to tell the world in a nut shell, in a separate book that addresses this.

You roll in the ball and the other side of the board has protectors. There are calluses that you get when you are being molested a lot. Whether it's soft tissues in your body, or muscle. Just think of a big callus – you can cut it and it doesn't bleed. Eventually, it will bleed again. My callus is running thin after trying to hold it all together. I'm very callused, but I'm tender underneath that callus. I have a callus that keeps me strong through darker roads. Your calluses can take the blades; you still bleed, but not for a while. You take it and take it, but when you start to bleed, you might get noticed and get help. You might cry.

The only reason that I got to Oregon (I was just taking it in CA). I met this ex-meth addict because I love to help people. She gave me her time.

I got a message from God, you need to help the children again. I understood the message to be that I needed to go back into pre-school. So, I started getting a message from the Golden Pearl Army to help kids. I looked on-line since I'd been missing my father, and I looked into Oregon. My kids got washed up like a tidal wave. I got the message in the night that I needed to help the children. Little did I know, I was saving children from horrific sexual abuse.

I was trained like a dog, and Larry had a severe fetish so that out of every hour and half out of a 12 hour day, there was a sexual act. The reason that I've come up with this is because he had a severe brain rot.

That's where I believe that the slayer comes in to be a warrior against the ball that's being thrown in to take out as many kids as they can.

They're talking about another universe that's right outside of this realm here that we're in. It's a star.

When I met Diamond at the Center, she said to me, "Cidney, shine bright like a diamond." To me, a diamond is a star.

I wait like an octopus for my prey. I first realized that I had a strange attraction to pedophiles, male and female, both alike, similar to the black widow. I knew that I could catch them and that I had blackout dark tunnels, but I also now have discovered that I have a mechanism in me that is attracted to them, similar to two seven year old kids meeting on the playground. However, if someone is hurting a child, I don't care how much I love you, the child comes first. It is very, very difficult for anyone who is in love with a pedophile. It's a constant battle of sexual adult starvation. Many will turn to food, alcohol, or adultery, who are getting no love in a sexual way. It's very hard on pedophiles to have sex with adults, they are really pulling through some deep issues to make love with their spouse. It's very difficult and there's a lot that can be done to help this. I know about this from inside and out. It's a vicious ring. When I'm a tattle taler, it's a pain. I watched my mother suffer many years from lack of sex.

From the list on the hand-written sheets (later typed up):
- Evidence left in the mind – everyone gets a mission and we have a mission map that we follow.
- Larry trained me like a dog. So, I have evidence in my mind, and I get triggered. I believe that there are people who have a sickness but they don't act on it. I feel for those people. I have mercy after living with someone so severely sick. It would be like living with someone who chops people up.
- Illusions of love – this is that my mom thought that Larry was in love with her. She thought she loved him. She had a baby with him even after knowing several times that she was having sex with someone who had sex with her kids. She will say that she is a victim because he beat her a lot. Larry was abusive. He did not beat her every day, but a couple of times a month, there would be a big fight. Her former husband was abusive to her, too. Trying to point out in this is if you have children, and you're caring enough to read this book, then you have been taught a few awareness clicks from the Golden Pearl Army. Men and women, if they are into children, they will

seak out women or men with kids to get to the kids, and not really even care about the woman or the man. Probably about 20 – 30 percent. Hate to burst the world's bubble but we need to figure out how to weed them out. Just be aware that you will find these types of lurkers in places where little kids are. They're in our school district, in homes, everywhere. We need to make sure that these people aren't after your kids rather than you.

- Hide and Go Seak – one of the games that Larry played daily. He liked to play games so that he could put me in a position for sexual acts. He would have an erection and dry fuck me. (Cuz it sure as fuck wasn't sex.) So, some of it was games. Different singing games and dancing games. Taking me to empty apartment buildings, and having me do different sexual acts in apartment buildings. He'd have me wipe myself down with a wash cloth.
- Booger monster (chaser)
- Hurts animal in yard
- His Irish Setter; they're hyper, skittish, etc. he doesn't have tolerance for dogs that won't obey him. The dog tore his marijuana plants up so he picked him up and threw him. We weren't really close to the dog because Larry wouldn't allow us to be close to anything but him.
- Cowboys and Indians
- He liked to tie me up in the garage and spread me naked from the wood beams in the garage. He'd be the cowboy, and I'd be the Indian. My great grandmother was full blooded Cherokee Indian.
- Consciousness /awareness (at age 5, saying, "oh fuck" in my head about Larry)
- He said "Hi, Sexy" to me when he got in the car. That's how we met Larry because my dad was best friends with Larry's older brother.
- Scary Monsters
- It was my step-dad, Larry, when he'd come into my room in the middle of the night. If I didn't hang things the right way on the hanger, he'd rip everything apart in the whole room. He'd tear it apart like a hurricane. I was so conscious as a kid,

you just get worn to pieces. But good things have come across because I've saved many children.

- Drunk Monster
- Dancing for niceness, sexual oral play with sister
- Left with Enimie – don't lie – sorry daddy
- Teacher (Miss Wood) in 5th grade
- Freeway Killer

When I was a kid I used to get in trouble for telling on Larry. Every time I told, I planned it and prepared. When I found out that my boss was a pedophile. I like to give the benefit of the doubt, but once it's there, I have to take you down. I had to get out of there by 5 PM; all my stuff moved out. It's like the golden shining pearl armor – they help me through all of the hidden tasks. Some of it is like being wet, whipped and hanging with rope. I'm so frightened for my life. There's a lot involved in tattle-telling.

--

I once knew a man who would turn off his porn whenever I'd walk into the room. I got a message from the Golden Pearl Army. People get messages from when they pray. I have an outstanding vibration of the Golden Pearl Army for children and babies. After I reported this man, all of a sudden, I could hear babies calling throughout the Wal-mart – it almost sounded like angels singing. I was being thanked from the Golden Pearl Army after reporting him. I got the message of "thank you." I got little gifts from the Golden Pearl Army sent down to me. So, that's about it.

The Golden Layered Onion: The Bittersweet Pain of Post-Traumatic Stress Disorder
The Journal of a Child Sex Slave
October 11, 2016

The lady that I am working with is 95 years old. I'm taking care of her. When I come into the homes of people, I have the ability to bring their power back to them. They become happier and more powerful. I do that through compassion, empathy, mercy, and what I would want done to me. The lady across the street from her noticed a big change in my client since I started working there, and she has mentioned it several times. My client taught me how to make English muffin bread. I said that we should give some to her neighbor. When her neighbor came over to get her bread, she brought a sand dollar that she had found on the beach that day. A couple of hours later, my client's daughter came over and we were talking. She said, "I went to the beach and I said 'God, can't you give me one sand dollar whole?'" Then she looked down on the ground and she saw a sand dollar. I told her that I had just received a sand dollar from the neighbor. The daughter offered to decorate it for me, and put a magnet on it.

I decided that day to take my dog, Blue, to the beach. I like it there because it has fresh water and salt water. I'm walking on the beach, and I said, "God, I need a bag of money." And I felt it in my heart that I was going to find a bag of money! I knew that it was real, so I started searching for it. Then my dog and I left. We picked up my husband, and I went to my mailbox, and I got a big fat check ($5,763) within an hour of asking God for money. I got it because the State owed me money, but I never knew about it, and they sent it to me. Then, that same day, I went into Chase Bank, and they qualified me for a $2,000 credit card. I was like, "Damn – wow! I got $7,763 after asking God for some money." Then, my husband got his check, and my check came in from the State. I took the money and paid off my cars. The lady who I paid off the cars also said that they had been praying for money, so I was able to bless them with that by paying off the Volvos.

Some people might look at that and say that's dumb…you were going to get a check anyway. In terms of my work, I had been putting out a godly effort. The basic thing is to ask for anything you want, as long as it's good, and not bad.

It only matters to God that we have faith in him, if we ask for things. I recommend it to the world.

When I talked to a child, he told me very seriously that he begged God to save him. He was only eight or nine years old. I thought, damn, the way I figured with the type of brain that I have is that God sends us people to get through to us as we need it. Sometimes, they don't always come when we need them, or when we think we need them. Because somehow or another Larry would get cleared, and the shit just got thicker.

So, as a little girl, I lived in California, and I went to Disneyland and it was my first time ever going. When I had my daughter, all she watched all day long was Mary Poppins. She would watch it full time at least twice a day. We also had art time, which I had for all of my kids. Mary Poppins – I thought this was a wonderful show for her to watch. We moved to Oregon, and had a crappy experience there, where they played on my innocence. After Mr. Monster resigned and left, which was about a week after I reported, I have PTSD anxiety breakdown, and it had me at every move. The more that I've been around these types of pedophiles the more difficult it is to get back out. One night, I picked up the story of Mary Poppins' movie. For me to get through that, I had to get through some PTSD and anxiety of my childhood. We're up in the bedroom, and my husband falls asleep and I put the movie on, it was the story of how Walt Disney found Mary Poppins. The lady that wrote it had PTSD. When my daughter was little that was all she watched. When I watched it alone, that was very brave of me. Walt Disney asked her to write a book about it. The lady reminds me of me. She had to leave her set, she would go into her PTSD trance, and leave, and go outside at Walt Disney's land. She would have to play in the dirt like she was with her dad. No one interrupted her. It's extraordinary; she wrote the book in her forties or fifties. I think, I could be wrong with the dates. It's a story of PTSD, but it's a very uplifting film.

When I saw that show, I felt like God was wrapping his wings around me in the softest feathers you have ever felt. My daughter had watched Mary Poppins over and over. At that time in my life, my sister called me, crying, apologizing for how mean she and my mother were to me. My mom and sister treated me like Cinderella for real. I'm glad that I was a warrior for my family. I'm sad that they didn't realize it sooner, and thank me for what I did to make their lives easier. I know that I can't go through life hoping they will change because all that it will do is disappoint me.

I am half Octopus, half human alien. I don't what planet to describe.

When you're molested, I'm only talking about sexual abuse. When you live it. You don't complain any more, which doesn't mean that you ever like it. What happens is that you start shoving these things down into your nervous system. When you're little it's like you're fluttering. Also, whistling helps, when you're a little kid, to release some of the pressure. It's like one muscle on a bone, and before you know it there is no muscle left, and all you sea is the bone, which has been sanded down. That's what it feels like for a child to be molested. It's a good way to describe it. Your nerves are raw which then leads to the mechanisms that you pick up on extra stuff – you're raw. When you walk, you creak, and every single effect is going to bother that bone. When you are molested some will go more introverted, and some will go more extroverted. I wanted to explain that for those that haven't experienced that. The pain is like a delicate knife that cuts you and it doesn't hurt, you barely know you have been cut, but the pain slowly creeps up and it gets worse as it goes. Your nerves are shaking, and you can feel it all. There are people out there that cut themselves. That is the feeling you have because it's in there. I'm able to go into that real good. By the end of it, all of my muscles were cut down. That's how I became an octopus.

Some of the things, since I caught Mr. Monster, it was horrific what he did. I have letters of deception; it was all a trick. What happened was, it took me really far back. Now, ever since then, I have been twice as badly off in terms of PTSD triggers. Long story short is that I have gotten a little bit better, but I'm not the same person as I used to be. When you know what's happened and it's clear, and reality stares you in the face.

I hope that this book could open the eyes of people who enable molesters to get away with molestation. If they do not report it and tell, then they should go to jail as well. Unless they really don't know. How do we address that in this world?

It's just another way for the enemy to sneak back in and get their fetish fixed. It's a human killer.

My mother believes in her whole heart that she was a victim. She also blames me because she tells me that it's my fault that he came all those years ago, because I wanted him back. Larry was in my life seven to eight years; from about the age of 5 to 13. At the end of my fourth year is when it started. At the end of my 12th year, going into 13, is when it ended. Thank you, God, and thanks to my father, who saved me. Sea how hard it is for the child.

The first time we told my Mom, is that I was trying to cover it up. We covered it up, when my sister started humping the ground. I tried to cover it up because I was afraid of him and afraid of the consequences. At the time, he did beat up my Mom pretty bad. He beat us all and spanked us all. Luckily he didn't do any physical torture, but he did mental torture. He'd put me on the toilet all night if I peed the bed, which I did at the time. I was wearing plastic diaper liners on my panties because I still peed the bed.

My mother and my real father weren't like that, they didn't do those types of things to me. All he was thinking of was how fast he'd get into my pants. He always made me take a warm wash cloth and wipe my vagina down before any sexual act so it would be clean for him. My mother walked in and she saw me down on my knees with my step dad's pants down and his dick out. So she saw what he was doing first hand. He left, but hat only happened once. Six or seven times, I told my mother, and he left. Five or six dramatic leaves because of the molestation. Even with that, my mom still put me on an airplane to visit him alone in Santa Cruz, California. My mom was always about getting rid of me. My mom believes that she was a victim as much as me. She left the court room when I described the abuse that I suffered. She had a baby with him even when she knew what was happening! Larry didn't have much sex with my mom. My mother told me later on that Larry did not want sex with her very often. That's because he was having sex with me three times a day. Duh, mom! My mom was always working and Larry was always either abusing us or watching TV. I know it's hard to wrap this type of behavior around the brain, the heart, and the soul.

I have horrific PTSD from being molested. I know that I repeat this often, but I want to make it clear for all of the children dead or alive, they never like it. If I saw with my eyes, and my kids told me about something like that, I would never let the guy back into the house with my children. I'm not here to make my mom feel bad, but I can't find any way to process her thinking. Was it only to find a baby sitter even though you know you are hurting your daughters? It's really hard for really young people to have children because they are not developed all of the way. My parents were both sixteen when they were having sex, back then, they did not have birth control. My mother said that she only had sex once to have me. If one of the parents leaves, the baby may suffer many consequences. The door may open to other men and women that are only after one thing: the child. It's not just a simple thing, it's every day, all day. Your kids are in jeopardy. You need to investigate the people your kid will be involved with.

There are many people who have suffered lies and rape. There is a story someone told me that a father had 8 daughters that he was molesting, and the dental assistant noticed bruises between their thighs and on their arms. They called 911, and he was raping his kids so much that he thanked the authorities because he couldn't stop himself if he tried. There is no medicine for it.

PTSD can happen for many years.

If we get the people that live with the child: parents, cousin, or grandma – if they know what's going on and they don't do anything. I'd like to pass a law, that if you are in the home and you are allowing it to go on, you're just as bad. Maybe they don't know that it cannot be fixed. You're born with it or you're put with it from an enemy. I'd like the enablers to have some accountability, if they know and they are allowing it. People need to be accountable. That might help a few more people. It needs to be looked at openly. There are wives and husbands who know that their sons or daughters are being raped, and that's bullshit. We are all responsible for the kids. Yeah, you're a victim too, but get over it. What happens if a kid that stays with family that allows the kid to be victimized. There are consequences for the world to suffer - innocent people will be hurt if we aren't careful what we allow our children to go through, they can grow up and have a lot of problems. They can really hurt others or themselves. Surround yourself with more than one person that knows about this battle to give you support and keep you safe.

My great-grandmother Viola was a wino and she lived in California at Muscle Beach. She was really good looking. She was a bit of slut. She wasn't the best of good girls toward my grandfather. I never met her. She worked the circuses as a young girl.

I never got to be with my real dad. He'd pop in every one or two years. Larry was very controlling. They knew each other. Eventually, my dad figured it out. When I was thirteen, my dad and Larry were doing LSD together, and that's when my dad said to him, you're messing with my girls and you'd better get lost, or I'll kill you. Larry got out and he never got to live with me again. He went to jail. He did a significant amount of time.

When Larry got out of jail, within 24 hours of getting out, he told me when I was at work, that my mother was very mean to me and didn't love me. He asked me if I'd ever got my cherry popped. All he could sea was me having his baby so he could fuck his baby. So he could have his little nest.

There are so many people who care about the planet, the trees, the animals, the bugs. What we need to care about is all of the generations of children. We need to love and protect them so that there is no more molestation going on. Maybe that is asking a lot. Maybe it can't happen altogether, or maybe we can't catch them all. When a human pops out, we need to treat it like our best beautiful tree. We need to water it, etc. Just like we spray our plants against predators. We need to spray our children with protection because they are us. So, I just want us all to be able to realize that the children are just as important as the trees, the bugs, etc. They are us in the future – our children are us in the future!

Why do we want the bugs to go away? Because we want to stay alive. We don't want them to eat our crops. In order for the planet to stay alive, it's going to be really bad later if we don't get the molesters away. Sixty percent of molesters have never been molested. I know we care about the planet, the trees and birds, but we're forgetting the child, who needs to be raised with love and goodness. Every baby born has rights to protect their journey on the planet.

I know that there are many good people and parents; more than there are bad, but one bad apple can ruin a very large bunch.

Pedophiles are getting away with this too much. That's why I'm saying this. If we don't take care of the next generation, who is going to take care of the planet, etc.? We aren't able to produce at our maximum abilities if they are being molested. We, as a whole, need to address pedophilia and get as much knowledge, awareness so that we can help our DNA.

The Golden Layered Onion: The Bittersweet Pain of Post-Traumatic Stress Disorder
The Journal of a Child Sex Slave
October 18, 2016

<u>Grooming</u>

At the time of Larry grooming me, he was so addicted to me and by seaing me, his brain took off and he saw me as his new woman, or lover...whatever the fuck you want to call it. You couldn't get him off of that focus for 7 or 8 years. I was a victim of a roller coaster child molester. I remember at the age of just 5 years old thinking to myself, I said, "Oh fuck." What I am trying to say, is that this guy is really, really bad; really weird. At this point, I can feel it. I can go back to my memory right now. I just remember how conscious I was of how bad he was, even at that young age, little people have a very big awareness of when the child molester starts to show its real true desires. The child will know in its brain, and then as they become more and more groomed, they lose their way consciously, their brain does. I was a bird with clipped wings, and then he opened the door.

We came to Canada to pick up my real father and we left with the child molester. I was there, but not by choice. He got in the car because he was my father's best friend's little brother. He had a way in and he took that way in quick. I remember feeling this weight on me, starting to happen. The whole time he would be lying in bed with my mom, he would be looking at me. I didn't have a way to explain it, but I could feel the wrongness starting. Right away, within 2 months, Larry was starting these games that I have referred to. He would have me ride him like a horsey, etc. He would have me ride his erection, like a horsey. He wasn't super old, I guess he was 19 or 20, and I was just going on five years old. That's when the play started, where he would lay down on the ground, and lift me in the air and drop me on his face.

By the time that Larry was 22 or 23, he looked like he was old, mean, and strong. And he had a zigzag man tattoo on his arm. Can you imagine he was mean as fuck, but he acted as if he was eight years old. One of the ways that he would be mean was to tear apart me and my sister's rooms. He would rip through like a hurricane.

This is when he started to feel jealous that I was ignoring him in the afternoon.

This was a way to get to me

So, this was a way to get to me. He would throw different types of fits. We would be in big trouble for really no reason. He would manifest things so that he could get mad at us, things that triggered his childhood because of his mother's obsessive compulsive disorder. He would blame everything on his mother, but 60% of child molesters have never been abused. At least, that's what he told me, that his mother was very mean and would put his head in the toilet and flush it because he looked at his little sister in the bathtub. He would often complain about not being able to sea his little sister naked. His mother would make him hang everything in perfect order. All of the clothes would have to be hung up the same direction on the hangers. That's what he would do to us: make us fold and hang everything in perfect order, or he would tear it apart.

At the time, I loved Raggedy Anne and Andy. They were my clock, time to wake up. I try not to let my PTSD take away my joy of Raggedy Anne and Andy. If I peed in my bed, Larry would have me sit on the toilet for the rest of the night. Fuck you! It was very exhausting. I remember sitting there, and there I was, obeying somebody who wasn't even my real family. He had got me. I was in his control, and my mother just let him do it. She let him be the boss; it was easier. I am not blaming her for everything, this horrible unfortunate disease, pedophilia, can hurt every single direction and every side of the coin. I remember falling asleep on the toilet. But, it could be worse. There's way worse people out there, but it was bad enough, all of his controlling behaviors. I know who I am with – do you? The man wasn't even related to my mother and she let him take reign of me.

This mother-fucker fucked me up to the point where when I got free from him at age 13, I don't remember much from the ages of 13 until about 17 – I could barely function the first year that Larry got out of my life, meaning that I was like a robot without the electricity. Someone finally pulled the plug, and that someone was my father. He saved me. The man who ruled everything that I did was gone. Thank my Father in heaven and my Father on earth that Larry, my stepfather, got taken out of the picture. I went blank like a robot; I had been trained like a dog, and my master had left. It was one of the best days of my life. The best feeling of my entire life. My real daddy came to my rescue; he might have been a fuck-up, but this was one thing he did for me and my sister, and for my mother, and for my new little sister, who was on Larry's list to molest as well. He was already preparing; making his little sexual fantasies in his brain so that he could function, while everyone around him lives in vain and in pain.

Cowboys and Indians

Larry tied me up from the rafters in the garage and did oral sex on me. Before that, we did Cowboys and Indians. I was caught. Well, of course. It's a game that they can do to capture you. It's like someone coming up to a little kid and saying, "Could you help me find my dog?"

Or, like someone coming over and playing games with your children; more interested in the children than in the adults. Instead of Cowboys and Indians, it could be a camp – this is another scenario that pedophiles could use to groom you through, with games at first, ending in a sex act. Bunch of kids go to a camp, and they slowly seduce the kids and that's how they get them sexually. That's what Larry would do to me.

For me, Larry knew he could beat me in the back yard. Picture this: Larry chasing me around the yard; I was the Indian, and he was the Cowboy who would capture me. We started hiding in the garage because it would turn into hide and seak. That game was almost every day. Not every day would I be tied from the banisters, but every once in a while, I would be.

How can you really trust or send your kids to a camp, and say to yourself that you're going to trust that camp with your next generation, a possible US President. You never know. These are the next generations. These are us in new bodies. It is so easy to be tricked. It is easy to trust too for some people. They don't have a trust issue. They don't think outside of anything other than a little area. Maybe they haven't ever had any trauma; they had wonderful parents and a good life, and they are not pedophiles themselves, they are not child molesters, so they cannot think of a scenario of it happening, and it is very hard on the brain and the imagination.

I try every day to be free and I am never free. I try not to think about the children that are being hurt, but every day I wake up and that's the first thing on my brain, is how I'm going to get more children safe. It is so fucking draining, not because I don't love it but because I can feel energies, and I can feel the child molesters' energies. I can feel the children's pain, and I can pick up on children that are being abused. That's not to say that I'm perfect, but I know the signs.

Hide and Go Seak

Larry liked to play games so that he could put me in a position for different sexual acts. Hide and Go Seak was one of the games we played daily. He would have me wash my privates up and down with a wash cloth before his sexual acts. And then, he would have me do blow jobs and ride on him, or he would ride on me. He would also chase me around the house, and it went on for hours and years, he would chase me with boogers on his fingers. I wish I could have just said, "Don't put your fucking boogers on me, asshole!" I could take so much; I had such a shield of some kind of an awareness that I could deal with him and keep him calm. Like a white widow with pearl armor all over it for comfort and strength. It is absolutely horrific. Sitting here, I can feel it inside me. It's like being in a cage and being made ready to be fed to a snake. That's how it feels every day; like being a helpless rat being ready to be fed to a snake. It gets to your nerves beyond your wildest beliefs.

He would lick me for a long, long time, and tell me he loved me. His beard was always very pokey, and it hurt; it felt uncomfortable. He was on the rougher side; mean and rough. He would dominate me. Sometimes he would have a little compassion, and I don't mean for the sexual acts, since he believed that I wanted it and I liked him. In his mind, he believed that we were going to get married. He was going to fuck me and fuck my kids and everybody he could fuck that was under thirteen; that was all the way from a 3 year old up to – I don't know where it would end.

He would be grooming at every child's age that he felt was appropriate for what he was going to do per each age of my life. At this time, we had an Irish Setter, a kind of hyperactive dog. Larry was very short-tempered and mean and grumpy and miserable. For a short time in front of others he could act well, but when he would get alone with me and my mother is when the true monster would prevail. One of the things that he did to the Irish Setter was throw him across the back yard and have him hit the ground, which was concrete, because the dog had torn up some marijuana plants. I knew that I had no way of stopping that monster from hurting the dog. It was almost like it was me or them. How could I expect my mother to stop him if I can't, because I am stronger than her, and I was five. That would just be one more way for him to get me to do more sexual favors for him, through his grooming process, to scare me and make me feel sorry for him. I never felt sorry for him; only trapped by him.

He would cry and beg me to take him back after he was caught, multiple times, he would cry to all of us girls, my mom, my sister and I. He did not like us to be close to anything but him and he was extremely jealous. He always would accuse me of sexual acts with men, as young as I was at the age of 10 years old. Once, at age 10, he had a man tutor me. The man tried to have sexual play with me alone in the room with the door shut. I remember thinking, "Oh, fuck, another one. You must be fucking kidding me." I was able to squirm out of that one. I don't know how I got away with it. Larry sat out in the living room the whole time waiting for me; normally, he was in bed watching TV and cartoons throughout the day. I remember how scared I was that day; when he gets so jealous, I would pee my pants. Oh, fuck, I knew what was coming. He would scare the shit out of me.

Don't think that this won't come back in some way. Treat the children with love and kindness. There is no tolerance with sexualness with kids; it's beyond against the law. That is so violating the human rights of a child. My passion for protecting; I want to save the kids. I don't know how else to do so, other than to write a book to explain how horrible my life was and how it has affected my future mental status as far as people labeling me. My whole childhood was not horrible. The first couple of years of my life, I had a lot of affection from my grandma and my uncle.

My mom and Larry went shopping – this is towards the jealousy area of Larry thinking that I was his woman. (Fuck you, Larry, you are in jail for life where you belong. You're okay, Cidney, you're going to make it. I love and care about you, Cidney. Love, Cidney.)

I stayed home by myself to sea the neighbor boy, who I had a big crush on. The neighbor boy's bedroom window was up against Larry's bathroom window, and I wasn't allowed in there because I wasn't allowed to get into his candy, which he kept on his nightstand. That was only for sexual play and if I took any, he would feel very violated. When they left, I went in there and went into the bathroom and stood up on the toilet paper roll that was connected to the wall. I broke it, and that's how Larry and my mom found out that I went in their room when they weren't home. This was about 10 AM in the morning. My mom said straight to me, "Just tell me the truth, did you go in there, and do it?" I said that I did. Larry knew that the boy next door's window was right there, and that I liked him. So my mom was real sweet to me and she said, "Just don't lie, and you won't get in trouble." Then my mom said, "I am going to the store, do you girls want to go with me?" I already knew that I was busted with Larry, so I let my mom and sister go to the store, so that I could take care of Larry. I sat down by myself in the living room and I put on some cartoon; it was about 10:30 AM, and I knew that Larry was coming. He grabbed me; he took me down the hall by the hair. I peed my pants. He spanked me with the belt. I just kept saying, "I love you, daddy. I love you, daddy." After that, he calmed down and got nice. He told me to take care of him. He made me suck his dick with candy on it. I took care of him and he got in a good mood, and I sat in his arms, watching TV with him, and he let me have some candy. I felt like a trapped little dog, but I had a relief off of my shoulder. He was taken care of now and I could get him to shut up. The hardest part of that was knowing he would come after me within two more hours from now, again. I thought that was an interesting thing that I did as a young child, that I stayed home and took the beating. Larry would be nicer to my mom and my sister when they got home. My sister would often cry and I would have to come to the rescue, and take care of Larry for her. He always took us together at the same time. It really took a toll on my sister. I remember putting my arm around her and saying, "I'll do it, I'll take care of it."

At this time also, after sexual acts, Larry would be in a calm mood. He would stay normal acting for a few hours. One time he asked me, when my mother was pregnant, if he should do sexual things with my baby sister that was coming. I knew then I needed to fucking get some serious defense mechanisms going on and I needed to capture him and to win this battle. I had a fight or flight feeling of personality when he told me that. I went into more of a warrior more and more. I was so mad inside, and I thought to myself, there's no way you are touching anybody else. I remember having an overwhelming feeling of faith in my Father in heaven and my father on earth. God gives children fathers for a reason. I promise you world it is not for sex. I had a feeling like I could conquer him. But really, I didn't, it was my father who did that. Otherwise, there would have been no way out.

My Pirate

In my mind, I always had a story that I really liked, and that has a profound story (Pippi Longstalking) she had a gift to help other children. She and her dad would go to sea, and they would have adventures.

It's very knowledgeable. When I was being molested every day with Larry – every day I was in some kind of trouble. To get out of it, 3 to 4 times a day, I had to do something sexual for him. Watching Pippi Longstalking let me know that my father was coming for me. I got the message. They wrote it for children. It was how I was able to meditate as a child, to get my father to help me. It's so invigorating; my dad's an asshole but I love him.

If you envision things, good or bad, in your head – that can happen. If you sea something bad, like a pedophile, you need to report it. It doesn't mean that you are always going to get the help that you hoped for, but if there is anything that I can tell you in this book, there is hope around the corner and it's lurking and it's on its way. Our Father wants all of his children to know he loves his little darlings.

My pirate is about my love for Pippi Longstalking, and my father came along and saved me. We went for dinner one time. My stepfather was there – he would not allow me to go to dinner alone with my own dad. My mother wouldn't go because she didn't want to be with my real dad. Larry controlled me at dinner. Billy, my father, my pirate - he came and he saved me.

When Larry was growing 8 eight foot high pot plants, and we had an Irish Setter. The dog tore them up, and he picked up the

Irish Setter and threw him across the yard on the concrete. I don't know if the dog recovered. I don't recall the dog after that; the dog did disappear now that you mention it.

Sometimes Larry would regress into a child-like personality. He would do it hard core –like a scary omen. He would talk like a child to me; an 8 year old in a full grown man's body. Sometimes he would say, "We can't do this anymore." If he would go 2 days without it, he'd become mad and angry. One day, he got so mad at my sister. We always told on each other. He would play us against each other in a childish way. It didn't work, though, because you can't break children's bonds with each other. He took my sister's bird and let it go free, and that really hurt her. But now that me and my sister are older, we can both look back and realize that no one belongs in a cage, neither a human, nor an animal nor a bird. I am sorry about that, but I know what it feels like to live in a cage and so does my sister. I guess that is why they've come up with the slogan, "If you love someone set it free. If it comes back, it loves you; if it doesn't, it never did." (I think it goes something like that.) Larry ripped apart our bedrooms. He'd do it to both of us, and then we'd have to put it back together. If we didn't do it all the same way, he would beat us and tear it apart all over again. He would come to some kind of conscious awareness of wanting to stop the sexual abuse, and then he couldn't and it would all start up again.

Bad physical violence and did not know how to handle anything unless it was being controlled by him. The child never developed, so the adult never developed.

He crossed the line long ago. That is something that was happening a lot. I have the image in my mind of him talking in the child's voice. I don't care about it happening to me anymore. I don't want it to happen to others. And as a kid, it's really hard to study. It makes you hyper.

The Children

I didn't know that I had the responsibility. I didn't know how big it was or how much it would take from me. I got more fucked up. I regressed back 100's of years. The slayer is an octopus. That's why this is so real, the Golden Pearl Army, and the slayer – she works for the Golden Pearl Army. She has the nerves.

Now I'm triggered and I can't live as fulfilling a life as much. I told my husband, I can't put my finger on it, but something is not quite right with him. I'm afraid he might leave and then when I come back from PTSD, he'll be gone.

"Could you give me 3 months?" I asked my husband, "So that I can let my nerves calm down." I work for the Golden Pearl Army and I'm coming out of a battle and I'm really really fragile. I tell my husband that I need to get away. I feel like he wants to make everyone think I'm crazy. If it's not real, at least I have it written down.

Minnie's Island – a lot of writers do have eccentric things like the protagonist. That's what I have. I'm writing all my fears down and turning them into stories. I told my husband that I am going to write all of the things that I think and turn them into stories and get them out of my head. What I mean by this is that I sea pedophiles that haven't been caught at work all day long, on the streets, in the stores. I can sea through them, even the ones that I don't want to sea. And then, I can sea the poor children that they are getting to and hurting and have hurt in the past.

Even when I had my baby with me, my last born, while I was in court helping them prosecute Larry Lee Dailey. The judge called upon my sister. At this time, my sister was 33 years old. My sister went up to the judge and looked at him. She could not turn her back around to look at Larry. I went up to Larry and told him to his face what he has done to me and the community, and everybody. The judge said to him, "I don't know how you got like this, and you cannot stop, but I'm giving you 42 years without parole."

God doesn't come in the first floor, he comes in the second floor, through the side door.

The Golden Layered Onion: The Bittersweet Pain of Post-Traumatic Stress Disorder
The Journal of a Child Sex Slave
October 25, 2016

I got the first sign that I was connected to octopuses when I was 13. My father told my mom to get rid of Larry or she'd lose the kids. He said, "You're not going to hurt my daughters."

Yesterday, I had a glorious thing happen to me at night. I actually got a validation from the other side showing my body looking out and in from out of it. This book is real and will make a difference. God sent me people to help me, and that's how I met you. When you have the experiences that I have had, I am so excited to sea what God is going to do for me today. Even on the days that I feel so bad, I can control my feelings of unhappiness and let go of it. But I cannot control God's destiny. It's not easy, and it might work for a minute. You have to trust that God will keep his promises to protect the children.

Where I am taking this is that I can't afford to look for glory for what I do. I need to make sure that the Center that I worked for, that fired me, is protecting the children. I'm not going to get recognition for catching the pedophiles. My reward is the kids' safety. That's my golden ticket. I saw a comic book again, and it's there. So, I'm incorporating my life, Pippi Longstocking's life, and Mary Poppins' life. This is a map to the Golden Pearl Army. My father is the leader too in it, because he had the balls, genes, and strength to stop someone from hurting his children. That's powerful. I don't care how many hoops he had to go through: drugs, genes, mental illness. He had enough genes in him to protect his kids. That is from the Golden Pearl Army. If you want to be on the side that is being on the Golden Pearl Army. That's why the moon, sun, and stars are golden. If you follow the light, the planet will survive. Kids have the right to a free apple sead. Every single being has the right to an apple sead. All I am is a beach bum; all I wanted was to shine bright like a diamond for the Golden Pearl Army. My daughters and my son might call me a gypsy.

Part of the map is when I helped the little girl, Diamond, at the Center. I took my family to Oregon within two weeks of getting the message to go there. Diamond is a little gal that we talked about. This happened to me after 6 to 8 weeks of working at the Center. I tried my best and I put my family on the line. I told my husband that he better leave now because I was going through the most horrific domino effect pedophilia - meaning many pedophiles in a group. The slayer is going to take them all down. God works through me and then I save all of these little diamonds. In the beginning we were all diamonds, but then there was corruption.

Diamond walked up to me one day, she was 4 years old, and she said, "Cidney, shine bright like a diamond." I shook her hand and said, "I'm here for you. Don't worry, you're going to be safe now."

Her story is that I had been working for Mr. Monster at the Center, a lovely school, it's pretty old. Pretty dark; all old electrical; pretty cold. That's where the children of the County go who are abused and who have hurt other people. So, they got kicked out of the school system even if they are 6 years old. Then you have some there because of their parent's addiction. They have been abused and then they go to school and they fight, bite, throw furniture, run away, steal, cuss, and might stab you with a pencil. So, they get sent to the Center.

After I'd been there for about a month. I came back to reality that I had moved my whole family to Oregon, and I asked myself why I'd done this. I went through massive background checks, because I had moved maybe 15-20 times in a 15 year period. So, I was sort of getting grounded again, because God sent me there; so I go through PTSD tunnels and then, I'm there. It's like an octopus puts his or her arm in a small cave to test the waters before they put their whole body in. They can look around and feel it. I walked in as an octopus, in Slayer mode, not knowing it, in Slayer mode.

I told my husband to leave me in the Center after it was dark, around 5:00 am. We were driving the company van, which we had the use of. I went in there. I saw a big slushy octopus moving through the halls like she was in heaven, and she put her arms in all of the rooms, and she tried to find out why I was here. I said, "Mary, Mary quite contrary, why am I here?" I am the octopus. I went there on a whim. It's because I am from the Golden Pearl Army. Rhymes are for children that is why that "Mary, Mary Quite Contrary" came out of my voice and asked that question. I went into the restroom as well, and I sat there for a second, thinking how fucking scary, that they allow one adult to go into the bathroom with one 10 year old boy. And they are alone with them in that bathroom. How scary for that child.

My nervous system was picking up all of that. Larry watched me 24/7, so my nervous system is like an octopus.

If you live on the side of your nervous system you become who you are. I am the slayer.

So, "Mary, Mary quite contrary came out of me." I went in the kitchen and when I turned on the lights, all of the appliances were broken. I was like, oh damn, you're busted. I was not scared. When Mr. Monster got there he got in, he was slumped over. He was a real live monster. He comes in and, picture, we've got 6 therapists in there. Mr. Monster is a marriage family therapist, there's also a psychiatrist, a social worker, two teachers, and me. I'm the octopus slayer. They don't even know it. When I sat there I acted like I was 18 years old, and I'm a very young girl in a 49 year old body. I was sitting there, and my own kind young self, and across from me is Mr. Monster, well, we're going to have our meeting now, and this is Cidney, who is our new certified therapeutic foster mother for the Center. She's going to be our foster mother. So, then they proceeded on and it was to have a meeting on all eleven children that they took care of in the school and their medications. Those doctors and those people sat around talking about what medications they need. Mr. Monster is all of those children's therapist. At the meeting, the psychiatrist, asked about 4.5 year old Diamond. Mr. Monster said that he was no longer allowed to pick her up and counsel her anymore. I had no idea that God was getting ready to have me be a Slayer. He had been counseling her in his office, and she complained about him that he had asked her to take all of her clothes off, and her sister, too. He wanted to touch them. She complained to her aunty about it. Diamond came in the house, and she was very mature for her age (4.5 years old). That's when Mr. Monster told the Board at the Board meeting that he's not allowed to work with her anymore. He wouldn't say why. He made it sound like it was a drug thing, so everybody just kind of went with it. Me sitting there, I was like, Wow. I had wondered where Diamond was; she just stopped coming to the respite program. I didn't put it together then, though.

About Easter time, he said to me that he was going to shut school down for Easter break, so he told all of the teachers and workers that they didn't have to come in. Diamond's family didn't know that the school program had changed. All he kept was me and my oldest daughter; he sent all of the teachers home. Just me and my daughter, Mr. Monster, and his son, ran the respite care. So here comes Diamond, and I said, "What the fuck, he's with Diamond." She said to me, enthusiastically, "Cidney, shine bright like a diamond." She's a real whipper-snapper that little girl, you'd think she was 8. I thought, Wow, Mr. Monster shut the school down and he's going to have Diamond here when he's not supposed to be with her. I could feel their energy and it was terrible. Right then and there, I still wasn't clear; I still believed in Mr. Monster. I thought he was there for the children's safety. Throughout the day, I tried my best to protect the children. To let them know that the way those people were acting toward them was not normal. They deserved respect as humans. Later that day, we had gym time and Mr. Monster decided to sit down on the ground, where we were all playing handball together. He sat down on the hard wood floor, at 71 years old. All of the 4 and 5 year olds would want to rumble around and play on his lap. He used to tell me all of the time that one of the groomings that pedophiles use is sit on the ground. So I, the slayer, sat down next to him, and so did my daughter. She didn't have a clue that the slayer was in the works. I turned my head so that I could sea both sides of me. My daughter was talking with Diamond, and we told her not to sit on our laps, don't sit on adults' laps. Trying to teach her what Mr. Monster would tell us, so that she could be safe. I could sea the other side, but having a conversation on the other side. I saw Diamond get on Mr. Monster's lap, and he had his hand on her, all the way up to her privates. She told him, mumbling, "Don't. Don't do that." I had to sit there and keep my cool. Elimination mode is where my brain was going. Unbelievable fear, because then I saw Mr. Monster with my own eyes. And I saw his son grooming this eleven year old boy with this very meanness. He kept him alone, and he was crying. They opened up the boiler room that day, like a dungeon, he had us all go out to play down through the basement boiler room, downstairs with little kids that have autism and are emotionally damaged. They never opened that room during regular school days. The son stayed with one new boy who had a lot of sexual abuse. You could sea it, and smell it. When the kid got out to the playground, he was bawling his eyes out. I told him that he had to tell. If there was anything that I could do for him was to tell him that he had to tell. He shouldn't be alone with Mr. Monster's son.

Then there were other boys, they would say, please don't leave me because it I am not safe here.

So then, I go home that day, and I stayed up all night. I couldn't sleep. I thought about it all day, and I realized that I was going to have to turn Mr. Monster in, because I saw him touch Diamond's private parts. Mr. Monster always said, "If you don't report child abuse, you will be fired." I thought Mr. Monster held the moon, but he tricked the whole community – or did he? I trusted him, just like the rest of the community.

I called Child Protective Services and reported what happened. They came out to interview me from the State of Oregon from Salem. Mr. Monster started to give me lots of letters. I have them all. I'm going to put them in my book to show the evidence of how he tricked me for about two and half to three months.

Three weeks went by and Mr. Monster was coming over every day, promising me money every day. He tricked us by offering big money. I could have given a rat's ass about the money. Of course, I wanted money to feed and clothe my family. I was so happy to protect those kids. I was struggling with not being able to talk to Diamond's mother, so I went to her. I was advised to not talk to anybody about the case. One day, at the bus stop at the end of my house, that's where all the kids were, and Diamond's mom was waiting for Diamond. She knew me because I was a respite worker, doing arts and crafts and I cooked for them. So, she knew me, and Diamond enjoyed my company. Both my daughters worked there; my oldest worked there, and my youngest volunteered there. I told her that I reported Mr. Monster for touching her daughter inappropriately. She said, "Thank you for coming forward because we have had other allegations against him." She said that Diamond had slammed her bedroom door, and her mom asked her if everything was okay, but she had to go to work, and her aunty came to babysit her, and Diamond told her aunty that Mr. Monster touched her. That was the first time. Then, I told her that I saw Mr. Monster touch her and how he did it. She said that is exactly what she told her aunt. I said, "I know it because I saw it with my own eyes." The mother was so grateful. I told her that I've been losing sleep because they have been bullying me. The next day, we met with the police. I told them everything I knew and what I saw. I told the police everything in the living room. I told them that Mr. Monster had told all of the parents that it was a regular school day and that he let all of the teachers off while he ran respite and that is where Diamond was not allowed to go because Mr. Monster ran the respite program, and he was there every single weekend.

One day, three months later after I helped those people's case, I drove by Diamond's place, and I got out of the car, and I was on the sidewalk. Diamond saw me and she ran to me, she hugged me, and said, "I know you." That's my payment. Unfortunately, Mr. Monster is still free; still on the loose.

I have witnesses that someone dropped off barrels in front of my Volvo.

The Golden Layered Onion: The Bittersweet Pain of Post-Trau-matic Stress Disorder
The Journal of a Child Sex Slave
November 2, 2016

How I was in school from Kindergarten. Basically, I was in Kindergarten and I wouldn't stay in my seat, and I was antsy and this was at the time that Larry came into my life. I know that I go over this a lot. My mom would always say that I was always a high energy child anyway, and they wanted to put me on Ritalin in 1971 or 1972, right when we were going to Hawaii with the hippy colony with a shit load of 18 to 23 year olds. My mom said Ritalin was legal speed, so she said no, even though my mom and dad were speed freaks. (By the time I was fourteen or fifteen, I was getting crank out of my mother's purse. I could focus and not feel so much pain.) So, I didn't go on it. My nervous system started becoming really raw at that age, because Larry was there. We were living from hotels and stuff, so I was under stress.

I remember being in my brain, I would feel scared, and a little bit afraid to go home, but I wanted to go home with my mother, but felt fear coming on around Larry. When I start remembering it, I start to shake. PTSD is also triggering me, but I have to go through it, or the children won't get as much help as they need. It's a low level, but it can escalate, similar to a nervous breakdown. I so desperately need to help the children in my heart and to help adults who need help that can't get any relief. I hope that this will help them.

I have a big huge bubble from Larry. I had to stay in Kindergarten for a second year. It was hard for me to absorb things. It took over my nervous system, which took over my cognitive skills. Besides that, there is the strength within me as a young gal, at this time in my life, Larry was actively laying himself in the living room, naked. I would be naked and my sister would be naked. He would watch me and my sister all day while my mom was at the pizza parlor. He'd lay on the ground naked and he'd lift us up in the air. Girls that age like to play with their daddies, but not in a sexual way. And I understand there are really good fathers out there, so please don't misunderstand me. I promise you we hated it in a sexual way. Even if we trick you to appease you in a sexual way, we never liked it. Even if they moaned because of their orgasmic body parts, they never liked it. They suffer in it and pray for help. He'd pick us up with our feet in his hands, and he would land us on his face, over and over and over and over and fucking over. It's not something to take lightly, it is very serious what was going on. I just didn't know what to do.

It's almost like you're sitting there and someone goes by and you think it's them. You think it's someone who is going to save you. It is very interesting to watch people pass you by like you are in a glass box begging for help and no one hears you. It is very interesting, God, the Golden Pearl Army, wants all of the children of the world to know that they have rights and they are allowed to by God.

Larry would also, in this same house, ride us on his hard penis, and I remember it so vividly. And it is like a fucking dirty, horrible, wretched scary nightmare. It blows me away when I think of it. There are people getting raped all over, right this second. Around the world, there are sites and people that are being raped over and over again. I know we can't save all of them right this minute, but that is not a reason to stop trying. People pay big money to go to it. These children are crying out. I am getting the message, I don't know about the rest of the world. There needs to be a new awareness that you don't have to be molested, you have rights, starting as early as birth.

That's what I remember when I was that age, hoping to God, and knowing too, that God would help me. I had to go through more to get to God, but the light was at the end of the tunnel, and there were stars along the way. God is real; God is around us. He comes in through other people's bodies, through other humans. It's similar to a good parent that sends his child off to school and wishes the best for that child but the child may still have a bad day and get beat up or bullied, and that doesn't mean that the parent did not love that child. He is hoping that other human angels will come through and do their works for others. Similar to what they call faith. When the parent sends the child off to school, they have faith in the school system.

Another year later, we were doing a lot of oral sex, probably in my second and third grade, I would leave the house all day long in

Hawaii, and I wouldn't go home because Larry was there waiting all fucking day. He would get so mad, and be pissed off by the end of the day. I had to deal with his temperament and that was hard. It took about 5 minutes when he was in my bedroom and I'd be there hiding. I'd stay away from the house, and I was 7 or 8 years old. I remember waiting for my sister to get out of school and me walking her home, on the way to Larry. Every time, she would poop in her pants, on the way home to Larry. I remember feeling scared for her and making fun of her; as most siblings do, we would make fun of each other. Even in Hawaii, my mother would be gone day and night, working and going to school. Larry would take showers with me, my mother, and my sister. I don't know how my mother could have stood that. Normal people want to have sex, and there were me and my sister.

It's so heavy, because I talked to my mom yesterday, and she said that I need to let it go, it's killing me. What's killing me is not doing anything about it – you're wrong, Mom. When those children are crying out, I feel them in my body. Sorry, world, that I've been like this, sorry that I've been a rat.

I want to talk about a rat story in our book here. It's a symbol of someone who finked. I've been called a tattle-taler, and I'm really fucking proud of it. It's like a fetish, meaning that I naturally obsess without even being conscious of catching pedophiles. I'm just now becoming aware of it, that I have a gift with picking up on their behaviors, and smelling it.

There have got to be monitors, almost like in a pyramid. What I mean by this is that there has to be people down here keeping an eye, and people above them keeping an eye. You have to have someone you know where we're all checking on each other, so that it locks in the safety all the way from the top to the bottom, and there is protection in the schools. Children will be our foundation. So, if we go, and there are 4 teachers and almost like stirring a pot, all the way around the foundation, and we stir the pot together as we teach the children of their rights and about no-nos, and boundaries of their bodies, all the way from the beginning of all schools. (This is important because children are groomed very young at home.) We pay for it from the book sales, and then the books will make money, and the foundation will give them the training that they need and deserve for a fresh new beginning at birth, of safety and joy. If we did 3-4 million book sales, the Golden Pearl Army Foundation can soar to protect the children's wounds and to lead them onto their next journey on this planet. We will incorporate it into the children's curriculums so that they have a very strong foundation. That's the foundation that I can think of to have a betterment to let the children know that they don't have to be sexual at home or with anyone.

I once read that a pedophile in one lifetime can have up to 400 victims (children). We need an awareness like no other. If we start now, think of all of the generations to come that will be saved from this horrific disease. In just a few generations, we could be up to at least 50% better, maybe more.

What people will be concerned of is that kids will lie. I don't know how to work it right.

My mom said that I need to stop thinking about it, and stop saving people, and if I do so, to do it anonymously. But Mom, that's not stirring the pot. And my mom says back to me, they don't need to know who you are when you tell. You can tell without anyone knowing. I, personally, have never been the quiet type, and my mom knows this, but she consistently tries to get me to be quiet. I said to my mom, "Stop, Mom, I'm here to help the children of this planet, and there's not a damn thing that I can do about it."

In Hawaii, it was becoming the realization that I was stuck with a really scary guy, and was manipulated by him for years. My real father was there, too, and I had a little power in me when my real father was there. He always loved me, but he was a drug addict. He did come forward and protect me after 7 years of waiting and waiting and waiting for someone to help me. I remember waking up at about 3 or 4 AM with twelve hippies scattered through the living room in the house, wide awake. I remember saying to myself, "What the fuck? How come nobody sleeps, is this zombie land?" I remember it like it was yesterday.

After Hawaii, it took another 5 years. When my dad left me, Larry was molesting me. He was so excited that my dad was leaving Hawaii and he could control me, my mom, and my sister. He got meaner.

We went back to the mainland, and Larry was molesting me

about 4 times a day with sexual play, rest, watch TV, and then sexual play.

At that time, Larry was getting more and more violent and possessive and one night (we lived in this apartment complex) he wanted to go to the play room they had there. He would play pinball machines down there. So, he wanted me and my sister to stay in the house. I was a 4th grader and she was a 2nd grader, and we just got off the island of Hawaii. He left and he was really scary. He had long hair and he was a big time bully. He said, do not answer the door. But we did because when we did, someone came and knocked on it after he left, because we wanted someone to save us, and that is the truth. I answered the door, and it was him. We got a good whipping for that, and then it turned to oral sex play. I licked my sister's side of her leg rather than do anything like that with her. I remember feeling really like that was going over my boundaries pretty hard, and just seaing my sister laying there made me feel bad, and I must have had to suppress it and get on with it, and get it over with, and take care of him. So, I licked her leg rather than her vagina, but he never knew because I tricked him.

Usually, we would dance all day. He would play the guitar and I would sing, but there was always sex behind it, all the fucking time. We weren't allowed to go into the refrigerator with him. My mother wouldn't mind – she'd let us eat whatever we want. He wouldn't allow us to get in the fridge at all. They use food to get to you – that's one of the ways that people can get kidnapped inside of a school system, like by a lunch janitor. (I know there are very many great janitors in the school system that have been wonderful to children, but we still have to be aware of the people that are taking care of our children when we're not there.) I put food in the foster kids' rooms and I'd let them get in the fridge.

Around 3rd and 4th grade, I had friends come over, and Larry touched a few of them. He got a sentence of 45 years without parole because he can't control himself. My story is legit, it's not something I'm making up as I go along. He already served 5-7 years for what he did to me and my sister. He feels sorry, but he can't control what he did. I have mercy for him; I have it for all pedophiles, but I have zero tolerance for the abuse that they can't control onto our beautiful children of the universe.

Why salute the flag if you aren't in it for the American people, including the babies? Don't salute any flag if you are for corruption of the planet. That's all that I'm thinking of.

I know God is real, and he's there. I'm so exhausted. We have to remember that the children are our army for the next generation. We want to build a strong army.

Who walks the school alone at 5 AM? It's because I'm in PTSD, and I'm not even aware of it. Let me loose and I'll find the goose. I'm a pedophile catcher. I don't want to do it, but I have to. I'm losing it, there have to be other people like me. I need them. There have to be other people who have the gift that I have.

Yesterday was my first day off in about seventy days. She (the elderly woman that I am taking care of) is taking a lot of my love. It's like having a big daughter or a big baby. The fear of dying is pretty bad. It's like being a guard dog or something. All I can think of is my father taking me out of that situation. Grandma didn't do it, your mother knows it and doesn't. Everyone was allowing it, then my angel comes and saves me, and that's my Pirate. Imagine you have a pirate and he is a good guy; he is an angel in disguise, and he cuts the rope off his daughters' hands and legs, and they can fly again. I feel utterly grateful. The Golden Pearl Army came to me to help me get through this and to help others who are going through the same thing.

PHOBIAS

I worry that my husband is gay, and I tell him that I'm fine with it. I would rather live with that than live in secrecy. But I feel this phobia. I don't know what it means. He tells me that it's not ever going to happen, and where am I getting it from? When I was a child, Larry would drill my brain with homosexual ideas, acts, and tell me how bad gay people are. I had loved ones who were really nice, as I have mentioned before, that were gay. But I guess in my brain, I worry about these different things that Larry would pound in my head.

I felt scared that my husband was calling me to tell me that he was having an affair with either a man or a woman. I get real sad. I don't call him back, but I'm living with it, it's in my head. If I tell him, he'll comfort me.

Sometimes, I want to be free from him because I am in so much pain from my PTSD.

My grandmother when I was 25 told me that everyone in the family knew that I was being molested, and no one would do anything about it because my mother didn't want them to be in her business.

Busting Mike was the best experience that I ever had, meaning, it was the first time that I became aware of my gift and my validation from the Golden Pearl Army of God.

I had to report my boss for kiddy porn.

It's something I can't do by myself, but I can write it down. I got a Master's degree in pedophilia. It makes you a warrior, a fighter. I did my job to take care of Larry, my mother, and my sister. I took all of that energy from that, and took it towards giving it to others who have been in my situation.

The Golden Layered Onion: The Bittersweet Pain of Post-Traumatic Stress Disorder
The Journal of a Child Sex Slave
November 9, 2016

In the message, I want to make it so that people don't have to stay in that relationship; they need to stop protecting the pedophile.

Summing up the layered onion, and my message in the book.

There was a lady who was raped by her dad her whole life. She came to find out later that he was also doing that to her sisters. My point is that I have more than one story of this. The mother says she didn't know about it, but this gal, as she grew up, had many, many problems. Relationship problems; self-worth problems. She never told anyone. She lived like this until she was about 35, and one day after we talked, she decided to drive to her parents' house, she told her father and mother what he had been doing to her all of these years. She faced it; and faced what it does, and lived in that.

Other scenario was when I was in the mental hospital for the first time, I was in there, and I went to an after program. I would go and stay in group all day long for 30 straight days. It was wonderful. I recommend it for survivors of sexual abuse to have this. It gives a new regimen of how to live without being raped. How it really is to live a normal functional life without being violated. It also trained you out of your negative trained old patterns. Then you also learned tools to put into action to help ease that pain, that anxiety, the fear of scary feelings, feeling like a little girl, with that voice within you. As your throat tightens as you try to take a swallow of your own breath. In the 30 day program that I was in, I met a lovely gal, who was about 10 years younger than me; quite thin, not quite anorexic, but close. I think she ran about 15 miles per day; maybe 6 to 7 days a week. She lived in a mentally challenged home for people who have severe brain damage but who can still function somewhat in the world, but they live in a very scary feeling. They have to live in a group home so that there is someone there to make sure that all of the meals are met. She was raped by her mother every day for 13 years, and all she could do was run, and she would make squeaking noises; they would come out of her in our group meetings. My heart was dripping blood for her. I wanted to build a home for people like her.

There are also walking zombies; they act, without thinking. Some have it really bad. It can seam like ADD, but it's PTSD, and being stuck in a home with a fucking scary monster for real. The pedophiles are the real monsters.

I was in a special group that my therapist put me in, a sexual survivors group, and I came across other people like me, who had lived with a scary monster, and made it out. It feels like you're in NY City and in an underground world, scary world full of rodents, and you get to finally come out. That's what it feels like when you have been stuck with a pedophile and you break free. If that's not enough to get people to start helping others, it won't hurt to help one another and to have each other's back. That will help our human race. Those that don't want to do it, have something wrong with themselves.

My basic deal is I'm not saying that I want to kill or torture the pedophiles of the world. But I do want them to stop what they are doing for the Golden Pearl Army. This is an obsession but it is a real live gift.

I hope that people are interested and that we can sell a lot of books to create a foundation. What would make people feel better is to hold groups, then the person can function in a happier life. This (molesting) is happening more than we want to understand. Those surviving it, who are coming out of it, are going to be mentally ill. We can make a stand that you don't have to live with this.

Writing books is how I process my fear.

Teacher (Miss Wood) in 5th Grade

My lovely darling teacher in fifth grade; no evil within her, she was in my life at a time when I was being at the max of my abuse. I was the teacher's pet (I'm always the teacher's pet). My brain was like – I needed saving. The Golden Pearl Army was sending people to help me. The best for the circumstances that needed to come out. They sent me Mrs. Wood. I would go to her house; back then they didn't have the rule that you couldn't do that. I remember, this is all I remember, and it pops into my brain every single day is me being a little girl at Mrs. Wood's house and wishing that I could tell her. Me thinking, "I wish I could tell her." I knew at the time if I told and no one helped me, and it went from person to person, I'd get a beating, and be told that I'd be murdered, my mother and my sister would be murdered. You know what's coming next when you tell.

She had a daughter and she wanted her daughter to play with me. I was gifted in math; I got all of the math faster than anybody. At the time, I had a tutor that my stepdad hired for me. The tutor and I were in the bedroom, and we shut the door so that we wouldn't be distracted, and he asked me to play with his private parts. He was 25-30, and he was really grungy. He did teach me my math. I did get away without being molested by him. When I left the room, every day, Larry would get very jealous and be waiting right outside of the door in the living room, in a chair, at my home, for when I got out of the counseling situation. He usually never got out of his bed area. He was up and out of his bed in the living room sitting in a chair when me and the tutor, which was his friend, when we got out. He was waiting and he was pissed.

This is when I was in Miss Wood's classroom. When the tutor guy left, Larry said, "Did you have sex with him?" This was every fucking day. If I was playing outside, he would kick me in the be-hind. He'd kick me and call me a dumb ass. He kicked me so much that it hurt. I was a little girl.

- At that time, you're starting to get the change of life. I was a little chunky; getting my features of a girl/woman. I was scared because for the first time I was getting scared. Usually, I could just manipulate him, and I could take care of it. Once I got it taken care of, I could do whatever I wanted. Right when I get home, I have to do it again immediately, or he will be very mean and haunt me. So, we're looking at every four to five hours. Probably 5 times a day. We always got a treat after. We either got some kind of chocolate, or some kind of powdered sugar with a stick. He'd sprinkle the sugar all over his dick. He'd rub that and chocolate syrup on his dick. At this time in fifth grade, Miss Wood came to my rescue. She took me to her home and let me have a play day in safety. I got an A in her class. My very first essay in the fifth grade, and I chose the Island of Hawaii, I got an A-.

The Golden Layered Onion: The Bittersweet Pain of Post-Traumatic Stress Disorder
The Journal of a Child Sex Slave
November 16, 2016

When my grandmother told me that they knew I was being molested, I felt so bad.

My uncle left me a mint condition BMW.

My mother had her pregnancy through her 16th year, as soon as her birthday came October 5, my birthday came on November 5th. Right around Election Day and the time we change the clock.

As an adult, looking back at my mom, I adore her to this day. I just loved and breathed her as a child. When she wasn't too busy, and she had the time, she was very loving to me in a lot of good ways.

My grandma said that she would get very angry if they would intervene in her life.

In the parking lot, my grandmother told me, we're sorry; we felt bad, but your mother would get very angry and jealous of my grandma's relationship with her brother (my uncle). She had me and back in those days, I think, in the 1960's, having a pregnancy, it was more judgmental than it is now.

My uncle was my mom's older brother, his name was Uncle Sam. My mother was jealous of my grandmother and my Uncle Sam's relationship.

I have 2 daughters and I have a son. We love our son, but I love my daughters just as much. How we treat them and how we hang out and interact with them, one may feel more favorable than the other. My mother was left alone in her teens.

My grandmother always had a Cadillac. I thought I came home in a Cadillac. My mom couldn't remember. I remember getting into my Grandma's Cadillac. She was a realtor; she was the number one sales agent of southern California – Orange County. She was a bad ass, and a chain smoker, and super skinny, and an amazing cook. She always had the pressure cooker on the stove for some reason or another. My grandma and my mom never got along. My mom felt like she was never loved by my grandmother very much, although my grandmother made all of my mom's clothes. And my mom worked in my grandparents' candy shop.

I always have very fond memories of my grandmother.

She once called Child Protective Services in 1971, before we moved to Hawaii.

My mother asked me in front of Larry, after she knew that he was molesting me; she knew it, at this time I was in fifth grade. Sexually, I became more aware of it. I walked out of the bubble. I had been seduced or groomed, for that time (I was 10), I met him when I was 4.5 years old, and had been under his spell for four or five years.

At that time, my mother asked me in the parking lot in our driveway in Huntington Beach, California, a bitching place, and I had a great time there – body surfing all summer long, and know my territory under the water there safely. I also did that in Laguna Beach for years. My mother asked me in the car in front of Larry, do you want Larry to be your real dad? I'm thinking, no, bitch. But I don't say anything, you think I'm going to tell you anything in front of Larry? Tell your mom, dad, and brother and everyone at the pizza parlor, that my daughter is being hurt and I can't help. That's all I was asking for. I'm dramatic because it's real; the pain is so real. That was the time I had to do a lot of sexual play in order to go to church. That's when I started listening to the song, "Jesus loves me yes he does, because the Bible tells us so." That's when I got knowledge of religion. I went by bus in a little old hippy church bus, because my family didn't do it, but my sister and I would go. If I couldn't go, the bus would come and honk, then it would just keep going - if I pissed him off, I wanted them to save me. If I didn't make Larry happy enough, his overbearing jealous insecurities, that another man was going to have me, were off the average human scale. He had such a strong disease, getting so jealous; or he'd get mad at me, and the way that he'd manipulate me would be through sex. If I gave him enough sexual time, he'd let me go to church. If I could calm down his jealousy, then I could go on the bus to church. To punish me and make me do more sex for him, that sometimes happened, and then the bus would come to pick me up and I would not be able to go out. He would not discuss it with my mother; he would just be the boss of it. The bus would come and honk and I wouldn't be able to go out.

It's almost like you're walking through a hard day at work. You can't just leave because you need to pay the bills, and you can't have anything. I don't know how I make it through the day, sometimes. I start listening to my body feel bad a little bit, and I will do a meditation; take a nap, and listen to a meditation, and I will take it in, and when I wake up, I can go a few more hours again. Then, I'll need it again and again.

Okay, now back to the Cadillac. The Cadillac that my grandmother drove. When she told me in the parking lot, I was around 23 or 24 years old, she was just about to die, that's when she told me, and they were afraid of my mom. It's very cowardly of them to let me stay in such captivity and know this. You would wonder how I became a warrior. We can know right from wrong, and that's how we become warriors.

My grandmother always drove a Cadillac. In this time, I helped capture the 10th most wanted man by the FBI. That's when I became aware that I could travel in my PTSD. I become aware – I'm 51 now – I have actual angels and people that come to give me messages, and I have them, amazing amounts. When I started working for the Angels.

They asked me to work for them and they sell Cadillacs. (That was a sign to me since my grandmother had Cadillacs.) They were white people who lived in Hawaii, like me. They owned a Cadillac shop; this is the letter of recommendation that they gave me:

> To whom it may concern:
> Cidney Harrington has been a caregiver for my 93 year old mother for the past 7 months. Cidney is very conscientious and caring and I would not hesitate to hire her again when we come back next year. She has been a huge help to me, not only with my mom but also with housekeeping, which has allowed me to spend more time with my husband and pursue our favorite pastime – golf!
> Cidney is completely trustworthy and honest. It has been our good fortune to find her! If you have any questions, please feel free to call me at (Hawaiian phone number).
> Sincerely, Angels

I'm from the Golden Pearl Army and Cadillacs are the special sign from my Grandmother, and then the Hawaiian phone number. They gave me a brand new set of golf clubs, and I got to play golf, and I love to play it. They gave me a golf ball marker; it was a symbol of the Cadillac. It's so sentimental. I am from the Golden Pearl Army. It was such a big coincidence. I felt very validated by the spirits.

My grandmother adored me and I forgave her.

When I got the message to come to Oregon, I was no more thinking for myself. I was praying, "What can I do for you, Father?" I sacrificed myself and I meant it. When I caught that man, I was so down. It was like stabbing me with a hundred needles. Because I'm an octopus, and octopuses do not like to be stabbed with needles with all of the receptors that they have.

In my head, the slayer lady she has one eye.

All of the billboards have the octopus right now.

God put me there, and to get the letter from the Angels.

The statement God wants to get across – he has angels do it for him. He has people come and work for him through vibrations.

The slayer is my original.

The layered onion came to me when I was 30. My therapist, that I had for about 20 years, Lisa, she raised my brain, not my body.

From the age of 0 to 4.5, I was not being molested. I was around a massive amount of drugs. I saw Led Zeppelin when I was 2 and that should tell you something.

Sexual pedophiles are not necessarily addicts at all. So let's not put the 2 together. I have compassion for drug addicts and pedophiles, if the pedophiles turn themselves in, they can have the serum. That's what's happening; it's going to be in books.

The first step - this time next year, we should be marketing the book. I want other people who have been in my predicament, they are still living with that pedophile. They don't tell on the pedophile. If you don't tell, they'll go to another child and the virus will spread. Then humans will be extinct. Humans can become so badly off.

The octopus isn't a cutesy funny octopus, it's a serious, battling pedophilia underground child killers.

The octopus comes out and it's coming out so much in my head, that I can manage it so that I can make a book. I can visualize it and the story. If everyone who wore an octopus on a shirt knew about this; they'd start to remember the octopus in my book; she's a lady.

After listening to the meditation, you will feel better.

When I did turn in a boss that I once had, I don't know what came of it. I never saw it. He asked, even if it's just fantasy, is it bad to have thoughts of children? If you have the thought, you need to report it, and then the Slayer will give you the serum.

The girl in the mental hospital that was raped for her whole life – she squeaked. She was majorly damaged, beyond belief. It's like a tight rope that winds and winds, and then it breaks. Kids go to school, and you can't judge based on how a kid dresses. You have to have cards to show the little kids so that they can say, "Oh, my mom does this, or my uncle does, etc." The best way I can think of is to do it through visual cards. There have to be some schools that will want this, and they will have the guarantee that there will be no pedophilia. Just like you can guarantee, you'll get a lunch.

I am such a party animal at heart; have a good time in sports, playing them.

Last week, I went to the lady that I'm working for. I have two ladies that I work for.

I was sitting at the 95 year old's house, and I said, I think I'm going to change my schedule to sea if I can work a different day than Fridays. I asked her, which day do you think would be good, and she said Thursday. So I went that day to tell the 74 year old, who I took to the market. We're all done, me and the 74 year old, and my daughter is with me, and we're driving back from Fred Meyer's and in the road were two seagulls. One of the seagulls was very crippled. The other was swarming around it, round and round. I felt it was protecting it because it knew its mate was injured. I just started weeping in front of my client and my daughter because I saw something that looked like compassion. Others could say he was swarming so that he could eat him, because he knew he was injured. My client just sits there, she doesn't get mad. We go home and we're standing in the kitchen and we're unloading her groceries, and she says to me, "Cidney, can we change to Thursdays?" And I was just shocked, and maybe it's no big deal, but for me those are big deals. They can come rapidly and sometimes they'll stop for a bit, and they'll come rapidly again. It was the same day. I felt like

I was being spied on, a little bit. I have been so much with being a mandated reporter, and the lies that I was told, when something was going on differently by Mr. Monster. He was making up a play and I believed him. It took me down a very long sidewalk. Mr. Monster would make stories up and tell me them. I would listen to them like I was 12; I would listen to his stories, and they were lies. I started realizing, when he called me a dumbass twice at work. My stepdad used to call me a dumbass and kick me in the butt really hard. When Mr. Monster said that to me, I knew, I started getting that feeling of fear, like I was a tiny animal and my worst predator was coming for me, and I knew I was doomed.

I promise you this, no kid likes it. Nope. They may have been groomed.

130

The Golden Layered Onion: The Bittersweet Pain of Post-Traumatic Stress Disorder
The Journal of a Child Sex Slave
November 23, 2016

My daughter will draw The Layered Onion for the book. She does pencil drawings.

Imprinted on the front, it'll read: The Layered Onion, the Bittersweetness of Post-Traumatic Stress Disorder: Survivor of Seven Years of Sex Slavery. It'll be black and white.

This is a true story of an event that was overlooked by the law, and hidden, and protected. That's the many different angles that pedophilia works. The people involved in it – it can intertwine.

In this biography, we are focusing on how the pedophile got away with it for so long, even when people knew about it. Why? Why are we as a whole protecting this and avoiding it?

My daughter will use the layered onion in her art class at OSU.

It has been difficult for me to get artwork from her for it, but she is committing to it now.

So many people will benefit from it, and that is enough to wind anybody up, right?

The doors open if we do stir the pot, and they'll open in ways you might not imagine, and maybe not the way you'd like.

These adults and other people don't feel like getting involved. I know how hard it is.

My daughter is finally committing to the book.

I have made a decision to study as part of my work, it's happening before our eyes.

One of the stories I have is for the comic book.

If I can commit to going over it for five days a week, and make myself work on it.

So, that's what I'm committing to start doing.

Some positive things about my mother. When the book comes out, and the people are exposed for their behaviors, it's similar to a karmic debt, and we all get it, and when you know you're behind the blow, sometimes people will suffer. It's kind of like being the tattle taler, or the rat. As a child, I was always the rat. I might even be the rat in the Zodiac sign. That does not mean, "You dirty rat."

In some parts of the world, rats are probably sacred.

To get through my day, if Larry did things, I started to tell on him. The only way I could get around it, was that I was the hero, and I felt that deep in my heart. I told on Larry, and my mother would say she's sorry. My point is that I was telling on the man who would do some nice things for me, and I knew that when I told on him, behind the blow would be my mother and sister getting hurt. Larry getting hurt.

But I knew it was the right thing to keep trying and trying, but for some reason, I wasn't afraid of whatever came my way to protect my sister and my mother. There wasn't a fucking thing that I wouldn't do for them. That same blow was when Larry asked me if he should molest his own daughter. He was talking to the wrong bitch that day. I have this warrior within me from very young to protect them; and he was my prey because he basically got life in prison. It took a while and some horrific actions, and I can't guarantee that the girls he abused after us will make it. It's a fight and a battle. It takes accepting some pain and giving it up, and saying, I can't run this all day by myself. Who do you go to then if you can't go to your parents or to your friends?

As the human, we are born survivors.

So, when you are the tattle taler, you're gonna throw a punch, and you're gonna stir the pot. Picture a whirlpool. That'll be a big part of a story in the comic book. A picture of a pot that someone is stirring. Need to sea the pot being stirred, and little pieces of different things in the pot. It'll say things like "someone not telling" in the pot, "someone trying to help" is in the pot, "someone knowing and secretly hiding it" in the pot. Want to sea the consequences of stirring the pot.

Down below are the children, the babies, and then with the pot being stirred. Somehow, we realize that we are sacrificing the human race, and the only way, it feels like, is for everybody to sea if it was in their shoes. Could that stop them from wanting to hurt someone else? It doesn't.

It's a brain problem that we are talking about here.

When you stir the pot, you need to have protection surrounding you. The way to get that is to go to a public place and you can actually sit there and scream for help. More than likely, you can get some help. But we get seduced and groomed for a long time, to the point where you're in fear all of the time. Somehow that takes over everything else when you're young. You'll be conditioned, and will stay in line. I feel for those who are waiting until they're 18 to get out.

The stirring of the pot is what a mandated reporter might do, or a Child Protective Services (CPS) hotline might do. That's stirring the pot. When I call CPS and have to turn in a person, it's difficult. You have to feel confident that the accusations that you are making are real and true. While you are waiting on this, the child is still going through hell. If you had it happen to you, then you know about this. Just depending on how bad the pedophile is, is how bad you're going to get it, and how many times a day.

A person that's a strong survivor will endure it, possibly report it, and there are those who are not as strong as others, just like a tadpole, that it is strong, the gene can make it, possibly reform. That's one of the things that I have done with my paradigms. As a person who reports other people for sexual abuse, the stress level of being someone who has to tell all of the time, as the pot stirrer; you never know where the Golden Pearl Army is coming from.

A lot of times, 3 different pedophiles, said this to me, and I thought it was so odd: "Why do you have to pick out the bad things? Isn't there more good than bad that I do?"

Two of the men that I've gotten have made statements like that to me. The second one happened to me in the Center. Mr. Monster said the same thing that Larry said to me, "Why do you have to look at the bad things?" At the moment, is when I almost snapped into a different dimension of PTSD into a dark tunnel where all I can hear is the children's prayers for someone to help them. It's like hands pushing through, help me next. It's like I'm getting messages from children all over the friggin' world. And having to know that I hold in my hands more than that many children that I've brought to safety. So telling on them really becomes invisible as a fear anymore. The reward is that I have helped that many.

When you're a tattle taler, people start looking at you and what you do. That's another way for that disease to get in and spread. It'll spread like a wild fire. Sixty percent of molesters have not been molested, but will molest anyway. Almost half have been molested themselves (40%). We have to conquer it.

People want to know where my evidence is. Mine is from the experience of living with one. In my opinion, for this to make a difference, we have to know the gene, just like when we know the chromosome or gene for Down Syndrome. If we know this, from birth, from now on – oh my God, how many children can we save?

Every newborn baby has that right to be protected, the minute that they're born. Mentally, if a person gets molested, it can affect them very much, to where they have a lesser quality of life. I'm just showing the world what it feels like in post-traumatic form.

Tattle taling has always had heavy repercussions. Some of mine were the barrels being dropped in front of my car and bike, and losing my jobs in the community. Being looked at as strange or a home wrecker. That's where it comes back to this. I promise the world that no children like it. There may be some that are under the spell of the pedophile, but none like it.

One of the positive things about my Mom – she believed that she could fix it. She had a fighting go-getter to her. She decided to keep me instead of aborting me at 16; so I got to come to earth and live on the planet. That was a big step in her commitment to keep me.

Although she was trying to trap my dad, the sperm donor (that's what she calls him). It was her way to get back at him for being a typical teenage guy.

She always tried to give me good holidays, as far as stuff is concerned. I always had expensive taste from the get-go, and she'd let me have one or two quality items.

My mother would be kind to me; I felt the lovingness about her, but it got worse when I became aware of my abuse and entrapment. My mother would blame me for Larry wanting me, and for him coming back to the house, after moving out. He'd move out for a couple of weeks for me telling on him, and then in a few weeks he'd be back.

When I think about it now, the pain of my mother taking a man back who was raping me; it is so difficult to even be able to like her, to be honest with you. Now that I'm a mother, I could never know that my children were being raped and have sex with the man who is raping them. That reality on top of the lickings, and the hands, the eyes, the punishments, the guilt, wanting food, wanting candy,

134

ice cream, wanting to go to Church, wanting my mom and my sisters to feel wonderful. My sadness that I alone would take Larry back, too. I wish that I could have gotten him away better from the other gals that he got to after me, my sister, and my Mom. He believed in punishments.

My mom, all and all, I can't feel any connection – there's still love for her there, but the connection has frayed completely. The deep love I have for her is still there, and she helps me as an adult, but her actions have been pretty bad for me. I wish that I could say that I have a Fairy Tale ending for my relationship with my mother. I have strived not to be like her. It's not me that has done this; it's her. I try to make excuses and have mercy for her, but there is no way that I can really even look at her very good now. I know that forgiveness is there, and I look at her as a reminder of how important the kids really are. She showed me how she didn't find the kids important; how unimportant we were. How there never was that thick of a bond with us. She tried to build one, but being hurt at home as a child – she had a high tolerance for this abuse of us. There is no way I can wrap my brain around it that my mom sacrificed her daughters to keep peace in the home, or who could have sex with such a man.

She sacrificed, knowing more than once, and as he admitted it. She wasn't well enough to protect us. She worked all day and night, and the kids stayed home with Larry, and waited for the time to pass to tell again. I would tell, and then wait for a considerable amount of time to tell again. Usually, he'd admit that he did it, say he was sorry, and then move out, and then move back in in about 2 weeks. You could sea his evil mean grumpy side coming out. After telling, you're back there again, at their mercy.

There was a pattern, which went on and on. It went on for 7.5 years. It went on and on and on. It was exhausting.

My family members don't really understand. Anybody that has been a sex slave, and you have to do things that you need to do in your life to survive. Some have had worse experiences. My family, it's been hard on them, in that I go over things a lot with them, like in safety or what's out there. I know what is out there. Not everyone is going to make it, but they deserve to. We can't ever stop advocating for the human beings of the earth; we can't let go that easily to the rope of protecting the children. Take the better road, which is helping the kids in the end.

The Golden Layered Onion: The Bittersweet Pain of Post-Traumatic Stress Disorder
The Journal of a Child Sex Slave
November 30, 2016

The paradigms that I'm changing in my life are helping my PTSD tremendously. It's a miracle what it's been doing for me. You have to hang onto it even when you have a bad day. It seams a lot to ask of us as humans, but believing and faith still work. When we are down, we can still keep plugging away and using these wonderful paradigm changes. We as humans are God's biggest creation. I learned this from Bob Proctor, as well as Louise L. Hay. They are both meditation speakers. When I was twenty years old, my mother had a book by Louise L. Hay called, "You can heal your life." When I got the book from my mother, she was finished reading it, I asked if I could have it, and she let me. It was easy to read. That was the age (20) when I opened the first book and knew that I could read consciously. They have been a huge relief for me to turn to, and to know that I am worthy.

Doing a small act of meditation every day, I strongly believe that it has helped my PTSD by 65%. I do more than one, and I unusually do 3 meditations a day, seven days a week. Larry gave me meditations of him of what he wanted me to be; he told me bad things. He subliminally, physically, mentally, did some mental brain training, but the meditations that I am learning now are taking over those. It's a battle on one side or the other. There are bubbles and pockets of scenarios going off at once. Depending on your fear of a level of imagination after being taken to certain levels of fear, you may have more triggers of fear than the average person. I try to replace his scenarios – since that occurred for 7 years. I have been doing it. I have been reprogramming my paradigms through meditation and I have severe PTSD. When I say it's bittersweet, it's because I have a gift with catching them (the molesters).

The Golden Pearl Army sends me cases. That's the friggin bottom line. When I was living with one of my clients I was having PTSD.

That's why I'm so passionate about the children, and what they go through. Nothing goes perfectly every day. You begin to let things let go a little bit. You have to trust a little bit which is very difficult. I don't have any trust; I don't trust anything. I'm constantly in worry of that, but at the same time, I know with everything that I am that my heavenly father is my leader, and I am his servant. I work for him and he will protect me with angels in every scenario I need.

An example of trust. Today, my husband put air in my tires; and oil in my car for me; he put gas in it. I let this all happen to me, being loved. But there was a part of my brain when I was coming in because the tires were too high and they were slipping.

PTSD – people that have to live in a community. If there were enough money from book sales, we could establish a foundation that would provide for that. Maybe there'd be four or five condos and each one would have maybe two people comfortably as roommates. There would be classes every day, so the people with PTSD could get tuned up every day. There would be funding for that; it would be free for them. I don't know. I don't want to be emotionally involved in it; I just want to provide the funding.

We have got a tunnel – the PTSD tunnels that go underground. You're little and you're in this world of hell. What comes to my mind a lot – children's hands reaching out so that I can pull them out of their situations and what they are dealing with when they are being raped and molested at that hour. It's almost like their energies are forming the Golden Pearl Army. I have this thing where children and their deep fear puts them in another dimension and in that dimension lies the Golden Pearl Army. So, when I'm in the halls of these dark tunnels, there are hands spreading out all over. As an octopus, I only have 8 arms, and that's how my brain adapted to imagine that I can help with that many more. I have a message long ago from a coincidence. The message was from my Home Economics class. I get vibrations to save and help children; and that's the truth, so help me God.

As I have learned to conquer it, I am conquering it. I pray that God uses me as an instrument every hour that I am awake. The quicker that I can get this book out to the U.S. and the world, then there will be more prayers answered, and I have served my God and my Golden Pearl Army duties. That's my PTSD.

Bittersweetness – it's sweet that I can help them.

I have coincidences to prove that I am part of the octopus. It may just be a portion of my brain; I'm not sure. There was the octopus that I made at the age of 13 when I just got free of Larry. It's fucking unbelievable. It was like going to Disney Land, and you walked into the most gorgeous hotel room of your dreams, with the best linens. I am a linen freak.

I got to school and I had a Home Economics class; and I made a lavender octopus. I had no idea that the lavender color and the lady in lavender would be so significant for me. And when I walked into a gal's house she had 1 purple candle burning and she was on meth, and she had holes all over her body (they were open wounds), and she was very dark skinned; she had a special gifted heart. She had some of the worst sexual abuse case that I've heard made it out alive; if you want to call it alive. When you're dealing with the addict there's no truth. But with her, she opened up to me quickly.

God doesn't mind me talking about this. I have to be careful that I don't boast that I'm more special than anyone else – that's against the law where I'm from. Where I am from, you're born with knowing the law. There is no taking sides. There's zero tolerance for sexual abuse of children where I come from. There's not even a 0.01% tolerance. They're in the light.

It's okay for me to share these things that are important for the planet to understand pedophilia in a different way, and for the world to become aware of it. It really is a secret way to damage the human race, that we as humans must stand up for.

If people ask why. It's the children's turn – that's why.

This family way of hiding it is not okay because then, who wins? The pedophile wins. They don't really care about you, I promise. As soon as you grow up, they'll get another one. They can cry and lie just the same. Wake up world! It makes you go insane.

There is always the hope for the paradigm changing. It's like an animal in a box, and they have a belief of an area. Sometimes it is so thick that the brain doesn't have anywhere to expand anymore. When you do the meditations, it starts to slowly absorb in there. Even if you don't feel like it, or you are in the darkest tunnel of all, you need to press the music or the meditation button and reach out for the help of that. In your pain, you need to write affirmations and put them around your house – where you are a lot. This will ground you and bring you back.

When you put a string around trees to find your way back. When you're in traumatic tunnels, you can read the paradigms to help you come back. However, for those who are not at that level, there is hope for them if the foundation has a curriculum that can ease some of the pain and fear in the body.

If we could have some small condos for these individuals to live at on a temporary basis until we train them and teach them, because they are alive and they can walk but they have to walk with all of this fear in them.

I really want to get it to where there is more of a complete awareness on a different perspective; on the child's perspective, what they feel like; how they have to live it in their tiny bodies. Endure all of this crap and then we expect them to grow up and run this country?

I want to help the world to become aware of their rights to be happy. Do the paradigms, whether they want to or not, they will make you want to drink less; your habits will change. The paradigms are in our head. They are the patterns in our brains that are taught to us. When you have repetition over and over it can get in your brain. I got that from the Golden Pearl Army, I'm here on a mission.

The first step is to protect; have someone report, and protect the little ones. I know that there is Child Protective Services and other foundations, but it is not enough. We must start from the very beginning.

I'm not saying we have to spoil them to death; we treat them with kindness. Children have rights. Every human has a right.

As a little kid, Larry would put candy by his bed side and he wouldn't let me have it unless he licked my vagina, or he would put it on his dick, and then I could have it. That powdery candy. Then he would let me have a few. He would do the same thing with potato chips. The same thing with going into the fridge – I had to ask for soda or any of his yummy foods, I would have to do sexual favors. If I was going to spend the night at a friend's house, I would have to take care of him first. He'd go into a vacant apartment of where my friend lives, and he would have me sexually please him there. He would have me do sexual things to him there, he would also be very insecure and needed me to make him feel that he was my only one. That was in Huntington Beach. So, after we would be done with it, the sexual stuff, I would be so glad it was over with so that I could move on with my day. At a very young age, I became very mature. I pretended that I was dumb; I played dumb – kind of like a dog plays dead, I played dumb. The same exact scenario; you could look at it the same way.

Now when I look back, I could handle his explosions better now. Larry gave me exact rules. If I followed the rules, 95% of the time, he would not explode as bad. Every time it was coming that time of the day to do sexual things again, I could feel a weight on me. Just a weighted-downness. It was so scary. It was just a scary motherfucking feeling. It never got better or subsided; during the act itself it felt very bad. It was a wretched repetition. That's all we did all day long, were hours and hours of sex acts.

Even at the very end, when I was thirteen, I was coming straight home from school. Always came straight home pretty much. We would play backgammon right when I came home. He stayed on his bed all day, so we'd hang out in his room when we first got home. Whoever lost, I had to do things sexually. He would let me think that I'd have a chance. My sister would play and I would play, and he'd put us at the edge of the bed with our pants off and lick our vaginas. I'm two and a half years older than my sister. Then after that, I could play outside until dusk. Then we'd eat dinner. My mom would be at the pizza parlor from 8 in the morning until 10 or 11 at night, seven days a week.

Larry wouldn't work.

We need actual steps to be taken. We don't need to give up on a case. Let's look at the victims, not the predators. Wake up. It's so simple, I don't know why I have to tell anyone. I don't mean to be rude, world, I know that there are people who do know about this. For the ones who don't know, it's hard to know because they don't have it in them to even think of it. That's why I am writing this book.

I feel that I have suffered for the children because I don't want them to suffer.

The Golden Layered Onion: The Bittersweet Pain of Post-Traumatic Stress Disorder
The Journal of a Child Sex Slave
December 20, 2016

Humans preach peace but the truth is that humans fight; we are fighters and we are survivors. We don't just always give up. Some of us might feel so down that we can't get out of that. Our mechanism has to be strengthened because you can strengthen the will to live. When we have children we want to stand up for rights, and protect ourselves. When we are little we can't do that. The adult can take over no matter what; there is no competition there; unless you get a kid that is really fucking smart who wants to fight to live. I admit that I have that; I notice that from reading my stories; I have the will to live and survive and to help others to survive.

The pedophile likes to keep peace and some will use peace as a manipulation. Meaning that they will say yes to anything; not stand up for anything at all; very appeasing. Even the ones that are the vicious ones and the dark that come out mean to their kids, but everyone else says, they were sooo nice. Sometimes peace isn't the answer, ladies and gentlemen. If we keep preaching peace maybe the little ones won't be able to stand up to it.

Sometimes someone who is too nice can be tricky. That's why when someone who is legit nice, people have a hard time trusting because sometimes these are the type of people you have to be careful of. There are good actors; they create an environment in some way or another that is appealing to its victim's friends and family.

In fourth grade, Larry was having my sister watch the door to let him know if my mom came in unexpectedly. My sister was in first or second grade. So, of course, my Mom walked in and saw me getting in the act of a blow job with Larry's pants down and me on my knees. That's when my mother found out eye to eye, even though we had told her previously. We moved out to a hotel for a little bit and when we were in the hotel room, my mom asked if we wanted Larry to babysit us, or someone else. This time, we went to someone else. Then another time, two days later, we told her that Larry had done a lot of nasty stuff to us. I was sitting on the edge of the bed, I was a fourth grader. I remember thinking, this is my chance,

I'm free, I'm free, I'm free! I told her everything that had been going on. She made me get up on the hotel phone and tell Larry everything that I told her. So, I called Larry and told him what I had told her, of the sexual things he made me do. He got on the phone with my mother, and he was crying, and he admitted it.

Larry was letting her go right then and there, we could have got out before he got more violent. But we decided to go back because we got tired of hearing him crying. The patterns began to start all over within 14 days. That's when all of those games, like the Cowboys and Indians, started. No offense to a daddy day-care; I'm not saying all dads are bad; I just landed a pedophile, so I became an expert on the disease of pedophilia. So, I want to share this with people to become more aware. I get along from day to day. I feel scared; I feel joy; I feel grateful; I have severe anxiety; I hear children cry for help. I have guilt and I have had two mental breakdown and many small breakdowns. I am not going to lie that there isn't a day that goes by that I don't sea the world in a different light. I feel fearful every day; on top of that, I have learned to go through the feeling and to know that it too will pass. The more times that I tell myself that, it goes by quicker, and I get a bit happier.

This feeling that I have about my mother is that she's like a really scary person to me, and the fact that I can't trust her, I feel wretched pain inside over loving her so much. Loving my mommy. But the letdowns, the mean looks, the evil eyes, the disappointment that she has over the years of my personality and the way that she raised my sisters to treat me bad, to make me feel like I was less than them, stupid, exaggerator, what planet are you from, she'd say to me all the way to the age of 45. When she said, "What planet are you from?" I agreed with her that I am not from this planet. I think it's so funny how our parents give us small clues if we listen to some of the things our parents say. They do have some information. I am so grateful and happy for the good ones out there. I am happy for the people reading this book who have had mothers and fathers, aunts and uncles, grandpas and grandmas or friendly kind neighbors, who are good to them. My mother knew and continued to be with Larry for another three or four years (after we threw him out). In that hotel room, she said to me and my sister that she was sorry that this happened to us…but then she went back to him. I didn't know that I could no longer be related to my mother until recently. That I would ever miss my children being molested under my own nose, is so scary to me. I let my kids be kids and be in the moment of childhood. I am not saying that I don't still love my mother and I understand now more than ever that she is not educated, but when you sea your child being molested and you go back, when you have the proof and you go back, the only person that it's hurting is the child.

The feeling that I had from my mother, and still, is the meanest face in the world. She never really liked me. She never wanted me. She got pregnant at sixteen. Then the man she got pregnant by, who was really good looking, was also an adolescent, and an addict.

The basic day to day for me was this scary man if he didn't get his sexual needs met. On the other side of him was a fun kiddish personality. As long as I did what he wanted, hour to hour, he was nice to me. That's how my day had to stay. I had to stay on ice cubes. I don't miss much, so now I become like a warrior, and I have gotten stronger. I know there are pedophiles around that I can't do anything about.

At the age of 14, I left my house off and on. My best friend, Cindy, lived in the apartments I had met her at when we got back from Hawaii.

Larry would call me "nigger lips" a lot. He wanted me to feel bad about my attractive self. What it came down to was that he wanted me to keep sex in my head because from him, big lips suck dick good. I couldn't even eat a pickle without there being a sexual play by him. One of the things he would do was to squeeze my boobs all day – for five of the seven years that he molested me. I don't know what my mom was thinking of not getting rid of him.

That's what I go through as the adult with PTSD; I worked really hard to be a parent with PTSD. I have had to trust my husband. The mechanism (to trust) isn't in me anymore. I can get to like somebody and I can get to know somebody, but trust is not going to happen. Sorry about that.

My trust issues since Mr. Monster have been exacerbated.

When people bring up the word trust, my mind seas fibers, and they're all ripped. I can heal certain parts of my body with my mind, and I practice it. I can't fix the button that has trust. But I can get to know people, like them, or love them, but I don't trust them, and I don't need to.

I always want to give my husband truth serum, so that I can ask him if he's really in love with me. So, I am going to purchase that. I can never remember or grasp that he loves me. I sea him day to day and I know that this is PTSD. My mother said lots of things and she left me alone with a pedophile. She might have asked me if he did it again, and I lied to her that he wasn't out of fear for her own protection. She got some beatings from Larry, and he wouldn't have sex with her. It was a shocker that she got pregnant. Pedophiles don't want sex from their wives very often.

What kind of people keep sex from their spouses? That is a bad thing for the planet, and the human race. It makes them get in trouble if they cheat, and it tempts them to be a bad person. They want to set you up to fail like them, and to be in like their category. For me as a wife, for my husband to deny me sex would cause PTSD for me.

If we have PTSD, we should write a little journal of ourselves, and our problems. Just write down a few things about yourself that you notice that you personally need to work on for yourself and others that you are around, to be able to get along with others. Some of the things that I do because of the PTSD:

Write down 2 things that you notice you might have to work on for yourself to feel better when you're in public and for others as well. Mine is trust, and another one would be I'm insecure. I may think that people think bad thoughts about me. One of the things that I have to do is say how much I love myself to ground me, because I'm all that I've got. I have to change my paradigms from my mom and Larry brainwashing me (oooweee baby, the things that he said to me, the sick fucking monster).

With PTSD, we might want to take out our pain on the people that we love; we need to be conscious of this, and not be so self-centered. Turn our worries and our fear into helping others. Moving forward, second by second, through those walls of pain, and feeling ugly and scared, like a needle could drop and you'd bounce. Take some deep breaths, even though it feels like shit. Keep breathing through all of the pain you feel, and get a meditation tape to change a few words in your brain even if it's just you are beautiful and you are wonderful. Ease into that feeling of someone giving you love, and you wanting to run from it. It's an uncomfortable feeling because we're afraid we might get used to it and it won't be there.

If you have PTSD, and you've sean horrible things - they weren't done to you - but you've sean them and you go over it. You could listen to tapes on forgiveness to reprogram your need for forgiveness. Everybody makes mistakes. You can change it the next time, and we are all going to need it sometime or another.

I want people to know some techniques that have gotten me through. Changing your paradigms is amazing. It's like exercising your brain to recover. You can have relapse but you keep striving and you keep walking through those little clouds of pain. And if you have to sleep a little bit, that's okay. I recommend golf, too.

The psychological parts of it – of the mother going back to Larry over and over again, knowing and seaing the abuse to her children with their own eyes, but she stayed for the convenience of child care. The pedophile is doing it. The victim doesn't even realize it. You can say there's black widows; brown widows; yellow widows. Pedophiles come in different types but they're all the same.

The pedophile; the victims; the mother. The mother and the pedophile are in it together. Even though she claimed to be abused too.

The pedophile will seduce the group; he would deny my mother sex, which would make her feel ugly, which would make her leave the house more; she's a workaholic. Then Larry could be alone with me more. He could beat her up because he was jealous that she was gone all of the time, and she had people at the pizza parlor that she could be friends with. He was cheating the whole time on my mother with us; in his mind he felt that he was the same age as me. He asked me to marry him when I was ten years old!

We were in the dark in the kitchen in Huntington Beach and Larry was cooking soup and he was telling me he wanted to marry me. I felt so gross. All I could think was, "Motherfucker, I can't wait to get you busted." Cidney was a good little girl and she fought and fought to be free, and for her sisters to be free, of pedophilia.

146

The Golden Layered Onion: The Bittersweet Pain of Post-Traumatic Stress Disorder
The Journal of a Child Sex Slave
December 28, 2016

Reprogramming the thoughts for PTSD. You have to pop the pimple and get out the puss and crap and fill it in with new stuff; so to speak, the pimple will pop and the hole will fill back up. It's so simple it's right there in our face.

The reason I know this is because Larry talked to me probably 18 hours a day of paradigm filling, telling me things, teaching me things, over and over. That's how I become a pedophile genius. It doesn't mean that they can't whoop my ass and hide it. People can be tricked.

Mark Twain is one of my writing heroes. I found a saying of his at the health food store that basically said, "It is easier to fool somebody than it is to convince them that they are being fooled." Mark Twain

When I was going through some struggles with cases with the pedophiles – catching them and protecting the children. Just deathly wanting to protect those kids. When your paradigms get changed from listening over and over to new positive thoughts, ideas, you heal for sure. The hole is there but as you do this you fill the hole back up and you take care of it. You keep listening and make it a goal to listen for thirty days in a row – that's what Bob Proctor recommends from his meditations. That's how the universe works; it sends us angels to guide us and help us. That's why God says, "I help those who help themselves." He has angels in waiting if we take that step. That's why I talk about the dark tunnels; if you can make it through them, there's praying and believing and there is hope. Some may still suffer, but I know that I'm a parent and when my child leaves my home, I'll always adore and love them, I hope nothing bad happens to them and they do no harm to others. If they don't, it's not because I don't love them. It's out of my hands. That's how it is with God.

He's telling us because kids are being raped, these are the steps needed for healing and to have some hope. This is some awareness. What I want to also put in here is that God, to me, because I've lived it, and I want to share it with others, is that God does not mean, when he says God helps those who help themselves, there is no anger in that; there are angels that are there for us. Just like your mother and your father. That is God's love. He wants me to tell the world that his love is just like the good moms' and good dads' love. That's why I'm trying to bring an awareness that no child ever likes to be sexually abused. All of the children that have ever lived or live would like me to share that they never liked it.

It's so important for me to let people know that.

When I was seventeen years old, or eighteen, I called Larry in his jail – the first time he went to jail for child abuse. He was there until I was 18 or 19. I was so seduced by him to the age of 18. I never felt anything sexual for him; I was always afraid of him, but I felt that I owed him my life, and his happiness was around me. I was very co-dependent until I was thirteen, for shizzle! When you are being held against your will for food, for playing, for opening the fridge, for talking to boys, for going to spend the night at someone's house, for going to get an ice cream cone, or just go for a ride in the car to have to get him happy after the fact. It all began and ended in sexual acts throughout the day, with things told to my brain. Thank God there was a caring judge that later put Larry in jail for so long that he probably won't get out in his lifetime. If you could only sea his violent mean side of him, it was scary.

I was skinny, and then I got chunky. I had to sneak and steal food from Larry, that he kept by his bed side. My mother did nothing about it. She was oblivious to the behavior that he was doing to the family. She was gone until anywhere from 7 am to 11 pm at night. She ran the pizza parlor. I'm not hiding it for her; she left me day in and day out, and that's when I was little. By the time I was 18 and her boyfriend came on to me, and she wouldn't believe that, too; she made excuses up for him. That was confirmation that my mom had a screw loose. She worked hard for me, but she never loved me. She always asked me what planet I was from. I told her, I'm from the Golden Army. I had to protect my mother and sister on levels that they will never understand, and that's okay. In the meanwhile, I'm not in the relationship with them that they are with me. I look at them as people who are small and fragile and can't do anything or stand up for their rights. Now, my sister tried. As time went on, my mother put a spell on my sister. I never licked my sister's vagina – she knows that. Larry tried to get us to do this. We fucking hated being sexually abused, we never enjoyed it; we just got through it as a group, her and I. It was hell on both sides of the sidewalk. When it came down to it, we were just doing what we had to do to survive and get to the next hour.

My PTSD and how it is kind of activated lately. I feel a bit down, but I'm still in joy because I'm so grateful for everything I have. I'm thankful that I can make a difference. I'm exceptionally thankful for my family, and for you, too. I'm thankful for God sending me all of the angels. It is extraordinary. I can't stress it enough how I sea the works of all of these angels all around.

My PTSD feels to others like over paranoia of your most wretched fears. You feel the fear over and above what other people would feel. With the PTSD that I have, I can pray really deep and come out of it now.

I don't know that prayer is the way for everyone. However you get to the light is the best way for you, even if you have to be on your knees with incense. Another thing is to have little notes on the wall to remind yourself of your goals and your truest desires, and to believe in yourself, which is very, very hard (believing in yourself).

I watched a movie called "Penelope" – she had a spell on her; she couldn't get into the king's family. It's like that. Once you fill those paradigms up and like yourself, so to speak, you can stay focused in your day-to-day tasks better, depending on your fears. If you fill the paradigms up with positiveness, you are less afraid; you have to break down those barriers. You can use those like gold tickets of strength. So, when you are in your scary, post-traumatic event. That's how I know when I am reversing – Larry filled my thoughts up with mean things all the time, calling me, "Dumb ass," or had rituals all day that would go into my paradigms, which were not healthy. When you start redoing them; people forget that they can redo them. It takes support, too. There should be a sponsor for PTSD training. The reason that I say this is because they help to gravitate you back to reality. So, if you sea someone touch a child and you have been molested, it will trigger you. My eyeballs are bigger, and I take round pictures instead of square. Why are pictures always square? They're not always square.

My main goal isn't about me. My PhD is in experience - in evidence of the work that I have done for the children; which is just a fraction of anything.

I'm just waking up every day, and following the light. I try to be as grateful as possible, even when I'm broke. When I'm down once in a while, I don't want to work. When I get there, they love my work. My new lady says that I'm a walking miracle. She asked me to stick around for 3 years. She's 88, and from Guadalajara. She is a very religious woman. She needs confirmation from Christ lately. Some people don't necessarily believe that Christ is the way to God. I have a relationship through the Golden Pearl Army to get to God for the work he has sent me here to do, and confirmation that I am pleasing to my heavenly father, and He always gives me confirmation, one way or another.

In the story that I am telling, I had a lady in lavender come down to me. I already know how God looks, he has golden hair with white there somehow; it's more a vibrating force of love in the structure of a human body, and he is so loving and wonderful, a being of energy.

God doesn't want to lose his people because of religious beliefs. Just like a kid in a classroom; what if the teacher is the one you should beware of? They know that they can take advantage of the child if the child is at home suffering.

One of my paradigms is the trust button. It is completely broken and will never be repairable.

It's part of my mechanism to catch pedophilia. I want people to know and that I get the message out. They are tricking us and it is right in front of our faces, and they're getting away with it. It's like a feeding ground, and they help each other out, and they get jealous too, sometimes. Larry would get really jealous because he thought that all the men wanted me.

I always had a fear of anyone; I could manipulate Larry when I got older. I figured out how to manipulate him. I lured him into my trap. It was like it was planned and I knew what to do. He moved out five to seven times in a seven year period, and came back, and as long as I did what he liked, I got food, treats. He used to rub candy all over his dick. It was amazing to survive and get away.

150

If I didn't have a mother who loved me just a little bit. She got abused a bit. But all in all, she could have gotten away. That is the hardest part of my PTSD is that I might let my children down.

It's a star planet; a golden planet. The only reason that I say this is that gold is the best way to describe it. It goes through your whole body when you know that you are pleasing to your heavenly father. We all have different fathers on earth, but there is one God.

Sixty percent of molesters were never molested; forty percent of molesters have been molested. That's what leads me to believe that it is in the gene or the DNA, so to speak. The molesters are robots; they only function off of one part of their brain. Do you think that they should be out in public without the world's knowledge of this? In a flood zone, it says "Danger." Having signs up for pedophiles should be done because that gives people rights. When I talk about it, I sea it and the kids. Like a war victim, who hears a boom and goes back to the war, well, it's the same thing for me.

It was interesting to sea the girl that Larry molested not wanting to stand up at all, and say, I'm so glad you've come to save me. She was so wretchedly depressed and suppressed. It was similar to seaing a war victim just walk off battle and get on the plane to come home after a very hard battle. She knew deep inside that there was always one possibility that she would be trapped with him again, and she didn't know who she could trust. When I was in the court room, I stood up in front of Larry and let him have it, eye to eye. He goes into little boy mode; he's not rational; he's at the level of a six to eight year old.

This is a disease, that's why I want to talk about the serum in the next book.

Anything causes my PTSD. If I'm around a family; I don't sit around and worry about the kid. It's based on the energy. From now on, I'm not going to hesitate and call on it. I will call on it every time. People will say, don't get in their business. Please get in their business.

After it's happened to you, you may have little bombs go off in your head, and you may feel like it's happening again – that's PTSD.

I have unbelievable things happen to me, and I will share it.

Think deep and look up, like an octopus down in the deep.

That's the only way that I have survived, including with the worst paranoia that I've had when working as a foster parent.

The Golden Layered Onion: The Bittersweet Pain of Post-Traumatic Stress Disorder
The Journal of a Child Sex Slave
February 8, 2017

I had a realization at seven that I was dealing with this kind of people, and a scary kind of monster.

If they came forward and told the truth today, at least we'd be able to protect people because they would be aware that they're pedophiles. He is known, he is a pedophile. But my husband says that they won't want to do that because people will kill them, which is true. But we can't let it be okay. It's their duty to come forward. I told my husband, should we let the pedophile hide and get to 10 – 20 more children? Or should we say, no more abuse on these little people; it's just not going to be okay anymore. If people are coming in from out of the country and they are known pedophiles, do we want to let them in?

One of the benefits of surviving is that I can tell the world about it. I want teachers to think about this as a game. You'd have a box. We have to figure out how to get these pedophiles because the children are the future. If we get too many together, then what will happen? What do we do with this? All we need is some kind of DNA testing to sea if it's in the DNA. I can't prove it because I'm not a biologist, but what I have experienced is that it's beyond an addiction; it's an illness or a DNA dysfunction that hurts the human race. I know because I have lived through it.

I want to decide on the closing of my mother. It's interesting how much a pedophile can trick and fool within one's own family. He or she can trick you; they set the stage, and in every direction possible. When we go into this book in the beginning, I want to make sure we put people into a new frame of mind. For them to be able to sea in a box and out of a box. I want to enlighten people's nervous systems. Pedophilia has the card of many masks. When you are a child, you have to sea the pedophile's many masks, and they are not fun, they are scary, and they hurt. They try to rot us one at a time, but thank God, that not all people who have been molested

153

become monsters. More people that have not been molested (60%) have the disease. 60% of pedophiles have never been molested; the other 40% have been molested.

Transgender people are honest with the world. They aren't hurting any little kids. My husband's Republican view of it is not the same as mine. All I care about is that children have their rights when they come to this earth that they are not sex slaves. I can't say that I'm going to stop it, but let's take some more steps and grab children's hands along the way. God sends his angels. He really, really does do that.

No matter how I wrap my brain around it, or how many times I try my best to give my mother the benefit of the doubt, she still left me with a man who she knew was a pedophile, who she knew was sexually attracted to her children, and she left me with him for a week at a time, for business and for visits. That is hard for me, as a mother, to understand. Once I knew one of my kids got assaulted, that would be the end of it; I could never send my child back to that person. So, my survival mode of having love and compassion for my mother, my brain clicks, click, click, click 24 hours a day trying to figure out how my mother could do this. My brain has tried every click in it, and it cannot do it. I look for mercy. My mom saw it in action, so there is no doubt now. That hurts. I hate it because I struggle every day with trusting a man or a woman around children. I make sure the child is safe and then I can trust a little bit. When you sea it, you know it. How do you still suck his dick? Tell me the technique. I would be so turned off. You put the kid back in harm. Where is the responsibility for this? I am hurting today because of my mother not stopping this for my life. She decided to stay with a man who liked little girls. She is at home doing her bullshit, while I am suffering. Thanks a lot, mom. Thank you. And, you keep me all of those years, from the real other side of my family. You kicked me out of my home for seaing my real father, you trapped me. You are just as bad. Her jealousy of my real dad not liking her, and her being stuck with having me, and her resentfulness. Such a deep spell and curse. So then, I became aware of God because if you don't have your own mom or dad, and you're suffering, you have nowhere to go. You run inside and there is nothing and then all of a sudden you have God, and you begin to know your mission. It's like the "I Dream of Genie" bottle, whoever gets the bottle.

There is a doctor who says that pedophiles are not very smart. I am here to tell you that's bullshit; they are very smart because their brain only thinks of one thing – how they are going to get to that child – BOOM! The doctor has his credentials – I'm not putting him down. He said that pedophiles aren't very smart and most are short. Well, that's not true. There could be a lot that are short, but Larry wasn't – he was 6 feet tall. Larry was a pedophile before he was even 18.

I think that all people come to the earth with a gift or a curse or something that they have to deal with, a mission. Part of the DNA to keep reproducing, to keep living. God promises that we will keep living, forever lasting. That's why it is so important to protect our children because they are us. We need to respect ourselves. That's one way that God stirs the pot is through the rebirth of us, for other angels and brothers and sisters to come and help one another.

There's also an ad to have mercy for pedophiles; that's the type of brain that is saying, it will never happen to me or my children. That's what that is.

I was speaking with my husband, explaining a thing about the pedophile and how there was nothing for free with the pedophile. I had to buy everything. So, the pedophile has only one motive: their selfish, sexual desire. Everything is about their need within their head. Everything has a price. I could not eat for free. I could not play for free. I could not sleep for free. I couldn't go to the bathroom for free. I couldn't have ice cream or chocolates for free. Every time I try to find something good about a pedophile, my mind shows me all of the evidence – every which way but loose. That's how I know that pedophiles only love themselves. They are only for one thing, and that's themselves. That's not to say they might not help the community, but there is always a price. They work for the community to get at the kids. What my husband didn't grasp was that it wasn't once or twice a week; it was every day, all day. If I didn't take care of Larry before going away for the night, he would go crazy, kind of like a jealous wife or husband. He was so abnormal. How they rationalize it is that because it's legal in some coun-

155

tries, it's okay. Doesn't matter what country you're from; I don't give a rat's ass, I don't care if it's Timbuk-fucking-tu, it's not okay.

For the mothers and fathers out there that have been told by their children that they are being molested, especially if their spouse is not sexual with them – that's a sign, the lack of sex. If they know about the abuse and aren't reporting it, they are just as bad as the molester, and they are allowing their child to be sacrificed. There is no cure within the family, they just want to hide it because of what the public might think. The abuse has to stop right when you know. How can you file an insurance claim on a car wreck and want your money, but not do the same for your child? HOW?! Why get car insurance – who gives a fuck? We just won't tell anybody because we'll be embarrassed. What about the kids?

The problem is – sorry that there are pedophiles in the world. Protect your child. You never know how the pedophile is grooming the child in the family. You owe that much to your genes.

The movie theater – it's almost like Night of the Living Dead dealing with pedophiles. They work their way into the family. The kid doesn't realize how they can worm their way into the family, and there they are. And they are stuck with them. It's by chance and fate that they will ever get out for years to come. Once a pedophile finds a kid they can nest on, they will try. It's so scary for the child every day. The school thinks the child needs drugs, but it's the home situation.

My mother got raped when I was four years old, in Costa Mesa, California. We heard a knock on the door, around 7 at night. I was maybe 3.5 or 4 years old. I had already sean a whole bunch of parties. My mother opened the door and there was nobody. She shut the door, and we heard a knock again, and a man came in with a panty house over his head. He threw my mom against the wall, and he had a big fat knife, and he took me and my mother to the bedroom. He made me stand there while he raped my mother at knife point, right at the edge of the bed. I had to watch at the edge as he raped her, and then he left through the back door. He was raping my mother, but he didn't want me to run off and tell. My mother had black underwear on that night, I remember. She had to go to the hospital, and I had to stay next door with the neighbors, who I barely knew. They took my mother to the hospital to check her. I'm sure it'd be in the paper if I looked it up. I don't think that they ever caught the guy. I saw this happen before I was molested. That had PTSD for me back then, but I handled it well. I had to be strong for my mother.

The Golden Layered Onion: The Bittersweet Pain of Post-Traumatic Stress Disorder
The Journal of a Child Sex Slave
February 15, 2017
Telling

Talk about how hard it is to tell on someone; especially for a kid. If a child tells, the consequences of that are big. They're afraid that they will end up having to be back with that pedophile, and most likely they will.

The steps of getting through telling. You go through a lot of things when you are a mandated reporter, or you're telling on something bad you know is happening to a child. You are going to go through stages. That's when you're going to feel isolated from the community that you're in. Not always, but you are going to go through steps of guilt. People making you feel like you're a rat or you like to stir trouble, or cause trouble. We're going to go through these steps and the pain and the punishment that the child gets for telling, and the adult that is telling, or the spouse that tells, and ends up back with the pedophile. He or she will get you. You will have a consequence and it won't be fun.

When you're telling on someone, you don't realize all of these consequences all of the time. You need to be prepared and to put your armor on, because you're going to get a lot of backswings. It's not fun or easy and you don't get a lot of rewards right away. What I mean by reward is the children's safety is apparent. What does apparent mean? Apparent means visual, actual proof right there in front of you. Those are the rewards when you sea a child's smile that they are safe and they can relax, and they can take a breath, and feel safe again. Those are my rewards. Those are your rewards. Sometimes, it takes months, even years to get a child safe again. There are steps of investigations. They can't always take the kid out of the home right away. Sometimes even, the kid doesn't want to leave. But I promise you it's not because they like the abuse. So they'd rather not even tell.

The other scenario is this: a way to look at something. Say you're driving down the road, and you look to the right and you sea somebody beating up someone, and you keep driving, you don't stop and get out and help that person because you say to yourself, I feel bad for them, but there's nothing that I can do about it and I don't want to get involved. You don't realize how much help that person needs in order to get away from that violent monster that they're stuck with. When you're driving by and you can't wrap it around your mind because it's never happened to you, you just don't want to get involved. You may even think you're better than them and that nothing like this could ever happen to you. It only takes one good witch to stir the pot.

This is about a little bit of a scenario of God, and how he made lizards. You can say, would you want to be a lizard? The answer is no, you don't want to be a lizard. Or, do you? Maybe you would like to be. Well, if I'm a lizard at least I get to have my tail grow back no matter how many times it's cut off. The reason that I sea it could be that God has the lizard's tail grow back – is when a good guy kills the lizard, he can reap the rewards from all that meat from the tail. The tail grows back because the tail is solid meat. That's one of the reasons why the lizard grows its tail back. Just because the lizard grows its tail back doesn't mean that God didn't have another plan for that lizard. There's a group of people that believe that man has some part of them from the lizard gene; lizard people; and it's not good.

Because actually, a lizard, if they have a lot of teeth, they can protect themselves without a tail. They have four feet so they should be able to walk and survive without that tail. The lizard's tail helps it get its victims faster and keep a balance. But once you capture the lizard and kill it; because its tail grew back, it is solid meat and it will feed the person that killed it. The person in this scenario is the good guy. I'm thinking of the lizard as a pedophile, because it is a predator. I am trying to say and show people that even if you catch the pedophile, they are still going to do it again: the tail will grow back. The pedophile will keep at the kids until it is caught and put to justice.

We have the right to protect ourselves; we have the right to know. My choice is to protect the child first. If you look at pedophile hater on the internet, one of the things that he talks about is the twinkle in the eye that the pedophile has. They associate it with a lizard. There is a uniqueness about the eye of a pedophile, and it is the twinkle. The lizard's eye is there, it is not worrying about what is going on. Pedophiles, they wake up and all they think about is sex and eating. Domineering and bullying the family, putting a mask on for all of these different areas of life.

We might pass it by, and forget it, but the wool can be pulled over the eyes. Pedophiles have many masks, even the ones who seam dumb. We have the responsibility of our own kids and what we put them by.

In this same vein, you hear people say, don't let anyone tell you, you can't change. With pedophilia, once you have molested someone, or it's in your brain and you're thinking about it, you're hurting someone already. You have that gene, period. You're not normal at all. It's something you need to address before it takes over you and ruins your whole life worse than ever. That's what they're telling you – to turn yourself in, to get help, but the truth is, if they get help, they will be subjected to bullies. Pedophile haters that want to hurt them. That's why they say, in jail, you usually get killed if you're a pedophile. And the pedophile knows this. Think about that. They feel their fear of getting in trouble so they don't want to turn themselves in, just like a child does when they've done something wrong, they hide it until they get caught. Pedophiles' inner children come out. So, if they feel their fear, they should know how afraid the little child would be. They are conscious enough to care about themselves. The only reason they do cry is if they are crying for themselves because they got caught. Should we have mercy for them? Feel sorry for them? Give them another chance? Just throw the kid out there for bait. The poor poor pedophile. We feel sorry for them, we say, they are sick. We don't want to hurt them or their families. We could just throw the kid out for bait. Don't let anyone tell you you can't change.

Many people feel sorry for the pedophile, or they can't wrap their mind around it since it isn't in their brain. It's difficult for them to imagine that anyone could do that. It's a sad fact but it's happening a lot and people are shutting their blinds because they don't want to sea what's going on. Most good humans have mercy, and want to help the poor guy. But remember the pedophile is not the poor guy, it's the child. We must stay focused on saving our children, the next generation. We don't want to ruin our planet. We're worried about the bees and trees; but we need to be worried about the children. If they are too fucked up from being molested, they aren't going to be able to take care of anything.

We ought to put a dent in it. I know it's not going to be perfect, but think about it for a second. Pretend you're five, and someone comes in and does something to your privates every day, and you can't focus anymore because your brain is not meant to work with that. So it screws it up. It's like a war battle. Soldiers come back from the battle. Most of them have some form of PTSD. It's the same with being molested. Most have a very difficult life. The more that they have a difficult life, the more that children will be born unprotected because their parents are mentally disabled. So, more children can get hurt from these corrupt people.

My nervous system, from Larry's actions, has been fine tuned to feeling everything around me, seaing everything around me. I can feel and taste things through my whole nervous system.

An octopus has nine brains, several hearts, and eight arms.

I think that an octopus has three hearts, and I can relate to that. That's how my first heart is destroyed, through the war of pedophilia. Thank God octopuses have three hearts. When I talk about the black heads, I mean that there are small pockets on the head. An octopus has nine brains to process all that is happening through its nervous system.

When you are being molested, your brain has to go into pockets because you can't stand it. You hate it, and you can't wait for it to be over, every time. It's a grinding chalk board in your mind.

When I was a little girl and Larry first came in my life. The conscious awareness that I had when he got into the car. Little people have very big consciousness of fear mechanisms. That's why we cry for our mommies. Once you've cried and nothing changes, you stop crying because you know it won't do you any good. Some parents believe that it's good to let the baby cry because it's good for their lungs. But I think it's good to comfort the baby. The babies are super intelligent and they cry to communicate that they need attention and love. Yes, it is difficult. It is not always easy to hear someone cry, but if we teach the baby that crying and pain and fear mechanisms in us are no good, and not to use them, then we cannot process our feelings well and we may have many many vices to

161

cope: food, alcohol, pills, drugs, self harming, and hurting others. We have to live with them, that's definitely not going to bring out warriors to have mercy to give to somebody else because they will be too medicated and wrapped up in themselves that they can't even help another person.

I'm not saying that because a baby is crying and we're driving, that we're bad parents. A four year old may be afraid to tell anything if they have been shut down a lot. Sometimes we are not aware of what they are going through because it never happened to us. Your good parenting can be damaged by a pedophile getting to your child. It's like when you buy a car and finally pay it off and the next week you get in a crash and all that good work is ruined. We use seat belts; stop signs, etc. to keep us from getting in these wrecks. We need stop signs and red or green lights to protect our little children; they are more important than our cars.

Stop and think about the rights of babies and children. There are laws for the birth of a new human.

Dancing for niceness

I want to put I love you, you're fucking beautiful. You can't always stop things. You can't always stop someone from running a yellow light, but if you sea someone in a car and they get in a wreck and you're a witness, you don't just drive away and say, I don't want to get involved.

When it comes to sexual abuse there is some kind of fear to get involved with that, and that's what this group of pedophiles is hoping for. They hope no one will want to rock the boat, or stir the pot. They want to put on one of their masks to give us what we need so that we won't tell. Sort of like becoming best friends with your enemy. What if you don't know who your enemies are because they put on a mask so good, you wouldn't even believe it. Forget the shock, and think of yourself as being at the child's age. Sea yourself at five. Put yourself all alone in that house with someone you are scared shitless of. You know when they're coming and you know what they want.

The Steps to Telling

Once you know, you know. Then you are a mandated reporter. You call Child Protective Services and you can either tell them your name, or you can be anonymous. You are going to be afraid and feel a little bad. You're going to doubt yourself, but just be a robot for God, whatever God you believe in. Every time, you tell, and you think about yourself at that age, and you be a hero for your best friend at that age. Because those children are our best friends and they are the future. You don't have to tell your name and no one will know.

You don't have to stop at that. But if you do go over to the pedophile's house, and you want to get them and get to the child, be meek, because there will be repercussions for the child. The child will long for you to save them, but not put their hopes in it. They may beat the child or scare the child more and tell them, you've told somebody; you've squealed. They aren't going to get dinner. If they are littler – the pedophile still thinks the little one is their age. They treat them really bad, so be careful in how you involve the child in how you're reporting, and keep an eye on them. Once you have reported, I think you can find out, although I don't know because they wouldn't give me the info on Mr. Monster.

In the community, some people will look at you. Stay focused on what you know is true. Keep going back to how you would have wanted to be treated as a baby or a young child, and stay strong. If you have to go shopping, do it out of the town that you live in, for a while. Stay low key. Act like you don't know what is going on.

It won't be easy.
It's never fearless.
It's the kind of fear.
You can't deny the fear
You can't hide
You have no one to turn to
You must be aware
Your worst nightmare is here!

You are being repossessed by God. He has no time, so to speak, left. He can't let this go on with his children. There is relief on its way. I can't do anything about consequences. Father, please help. You sea when I am in the tunnels, I sea the devil's work. I am actually here now, and people are all in on it in this town, they call Hell. And it seams like people are your enemy, but they're not. They want

to be saved. They cry to find out when is it my turn, Father, to end this suffering? You have to stand and watch everyone suffer. Because you know Hell so well, you understand the people that live there. So you can live there, play there, sleep there, and try to get out as fast as you got there. We reap what we sow, and I'm making a quilt. I never could understand why I had an attraction to quilts. My golly gee, I do know.

The Golden Layered Onion: The Bittersweet Pain of Post-Traumatic Stress Disorder
The Journal of a Child Sex Slave
February 22, 2017

We focus on the act but what I mean is that what happens secondarily is even worse to live with than the actual act because it's not complete in your brain yet. All of a sudden your brain starts to unfold. What I mean by this is all of the memories in your brain, without you even thinking about it are constantly responding to all of the abuse that is stored in there. It starts to click, click, click, putting it all together and the memories are in there like a maze. Every single spot you try to get to the end, there is always a creeping memory, feeling, smell, taste, at every corner. Put your hand out and ask God for help, and I promise he will deliver. It may not be on our time frame, but I promise it will happen. God will respond to your needs every time. You have to think about it as God is the cook and he is stirring the pot and he seas what needs to be done as he stirs. I have severe PTSD. It's like a black head that needs to be cleaned.

The Golden Layered Onion: The Bittersweet Pain of Post-Traumatic Stress Disorder
The Journal of a Child Sex Slave
July 22, 2017

A funny thing happened. I noticed aw recently on a cabinet made of metal from probably the 1960's, that I bought at a thrift store, that you could put hundreds of magnets on it, which I did not realize until I got home and discovered that, wow, I could put magnets on it. After having this cabinet for 8 months, I noticed a business card in a slot in one of the drawers. On the one side it said one of my client's name, and when I turned the card over, it had my other client's name. Then, on the other side of the business card it said, Sacramento, California. And the business card is probably about 40 years old, and I thought it was a wonderful, fabulous coincidence.

When I was 13, just as I was adjusting to my freedom of Larry being out of my life, I started spiraling out of consciousness, and I started young, even 13, wanting to try mushrooms. I was open to it, willing to ditch school for it, and already trying marijuana joints. No one had to twist my arm, let's just put it that way. By the time that I was 14, I was going to L.A. to The Starwood and The Whiskey, with my best friend, who was 18. She would pick me up on a school night usually, and I would leave my house at night and be gone. I would do qualudes and downers, any kind of downers. I would sniff this type of liquid in a little brown glass vial that would make me dizzy (and I hate to get dizzy, by the way). I was just trying to make it. I would go to The Starwood, I would go to sea Rodney on the Rock, he was a legendary punk music announcer. By this time, I had already shaved my hair off my head. I had long beautiful gorgeous hair, and I shaved it like a skinhead. By the time that I was 14 and a half, I moved out of my house and lived in the back of a car, and I worked at a fast food restaurant called "Jack in the Box." I started doing black beauties, crank, lots of alcohol, and LSD. Within about 2 months of using LSD, I was up to 4 to 5 hits a day of it. I once tried to shoot up but they couldn't find my vein, and I was going to shoot up cocaine.

I moved out of my house with my mother. I was not an easy teenager. I was very loving to my mother at all times. Only once in a while did I lose my temper, if my mom hit me or slapped me. But she rarely laid a hand on me. One time, around this age, I got out of a van at night with a whole bunch of guys in the van and I was the only girl. My mother was waiting and she beat me to a pulp. I let her, because I could whip my mother's ass any day of the week. I had so much anger in me by the time I was finally freed from Larry that I exploded. I drank every day, then at 15, I started doing coke. I got it for free. I never had enough of it, and then I got ahold of crank and instead of snorting it because I felt guilty for hurting my nose, I started drinking it in my coffee for about three years. There was a whole straight year that I used it to function.

I slept in the Laundromat of my best friend's apartment complex. I lived from house to house. I went back home. My mother let me come back home and gave me a small closet under the staircase to sleep in. She let me live in it. My sisters lived in the rooms upstairs with my mother. Then she gave me the garage, and by the time that I was 18, I started getting off of the drugs. I just would smoke a little bit of pot; do a bit of coke here and there, and I drank a lot still, regularly, every single day.

I had a violent temper. I would throw plates across the room. I would try to tell my mother about how I was feeling depressed and I was very hyper, but I was a hard worker and honest most of the time to the ones that I love. I got better at that now. Now I am always honest to the ones that I love. I remember once my husband saying, why do you have to be so damn loyal? When he met me, I had a boyfriend that I was with for seven years, who I wanted to marry and have a family with, but I could never get him on board. His mother would make fun of me, saying you don't want to marry a person that has been this abused. You don't want to be with a girl who has been sexually abused this badly. I remember being categorized as weird, quirky, eccentric, hyperactive, and I wore my heart on my sleeve at a very young age. Everybody I met all my life, after Larry left me, I would tell every person I met that I had been molested for years, and I am free. My mother would always say, why do you have to tell everyone your life story? I came to realize later in life that it was almost like my mouth was open wide and razor blades were coming out that were stuck inside of me. The razor blades stuck inside me, hurt myself, feeling alone and scared. Guilty feeling. Walking streets alone.

When I was 17 or 18, and this older gentleman, I was on a corner of the Pacific Coast highway, I was just leaving a boyfriend's house that I had spent the night at and was going to take the bus home from one part of the coast of Cali to the next. I was on the corner and this gentleman pulled over in a Mercedes. He was probably 75 to 80 years old, and he told me he was a photographer, and he asked if I needed a ride, and said that I could be in a magazine. He had my number. He knew exactly what I wanted to hear. So, I got in his car and we were about an hour from our destination, and he said, "Do you want to be in a magazine and be a model?" I had the body for that. He had no idea who he was dealing with when I got in the car. By the time we got down half our destination, he had talked me into getting in a hotel room by the beach to look at my body, he said. We got to the hotel, he went and got the room. Inside of me, I felt scared, taking a risk, worried that I might get caught. Just feeling guilty and bad, I could feel it in there, but I was ignoring it. We got up to the room. I had my clothes off within 4 to 5 minutes, I was completely naked, and he got into the bed. He came before I could even get the covers over me. I was so relieved – how lucky can you get! He got up out of the bed and went straight to the bathroom. While he was in there, I robbed him dry. I think I stole about $130 out of his wallet – I took all that out. Quickly, the bullshit photography session was over. We went down to the car. Oh, and by the way, he didn't offer me a dime for my services; not a fucking dime. He took me another 30 minute drive to where my mother's pizza parlor was. I got out of the car, and said, "Thank you for the ride." I went inside the pizza parlor and had pizza and money for the day. Even though I was raped three years prior to that, I still took the great risk to not give a fuck about Cidney.

Crops

When we take care of our crops, we start with a sead because in the future, we're going to eat it. So, we want it to be delicious, plentiful, so nurtured. We have to nurture our crops with love, which is water and sun, and having the knowledge to know where to plant our crops. We want to know that they are safe during the day, meaning that they need enough sun during certain hours. They need protection from predators. Why? Hmmm. We use pesticides

169

to protect our crops. If we use an untrusted bad brand, it could get into our systems and hurt and kills us. We want to protect our crops, so we use healthy pesticides. We try to think of new ways to keep our crops safe. That's what we need to do for the children. It's time to make new alternative, healthy ways of protecting them, whether or not the pedophile's family or other people might get upset over talking about what is happening to our children sexually. They will say, "Don't talk about that. Don't listen to that. Don't get involved." That's not the way we can protect our crops, because they are our future. It just is so clear that we can't sea it. That's why the Golden Pearl Army has come here to sprinkle golden pearl dust to sprinkle on the things that are so clear that we cannot sea them. Golden Pearl Army (GPA).

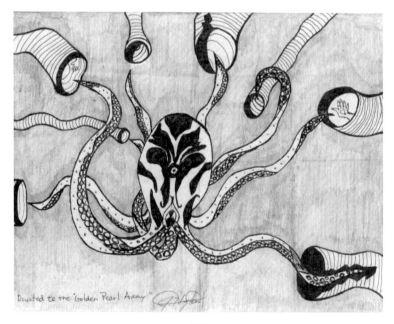

170

The Golden Layered Onion: The Bittersweet Pain of Post-Traumatic Stress Disorder -
The Journal of a Child Sex Slave
August 19, 2017

The Golden Pearl Army Island is a beautiful sea shore where God lives. The sand is not sand, it is all pearls. The whole entire sea shore, the beach, is solid pearls, some crushed, some whole, they are soft so they don't hurt God's feet when he stands or walks there, because he paces up and down his beach. The water around it washes up against the pearls and you can hear it almost sounds as if it is a light soft, crackling glass. It is soft and gentle. The water is perfect. It's aqua green. It's unfucking believable. (Hee hee ha ha.) When the water washes up and gently back down you can sea pearls all over. It's very very serene. You walk up and there are gigantic stone white buildings. A gigantic stone estate, and you walk up it into where God lives. He comes down the stairs onto his pearl beach. There are many beings living there. There is an army of God's armor there that are chosen, and they live there, but they live, and come and go to the missions that God sends us on. The Golden Pearl Army is the most important army armor of God's planet because it helps the children, who are us.

We get to swim in that water and it just feeds us. I know that it's where I'm from – I'm from the Golden Pearl Island. I finally discovered it, to tell people about God and how beautiful he is. I can't tell the world enough how much God loves us. Every one of us. We all have our own way of getting to Him. God loves even the weakest human there is on the earth; he loves every one of them. It's just like a Mother or Father who loves their child, and anything that their child is. They love them and want to protect their child. Even parents who have children who grow up to be pedophiles. Those parents, they weep and they keep trying to figure it out, but eventually the pedophile will submit to it and will forget that he is even a pedophile as he is grooming his next victim. Some learn to manage themselves, but all in all, they are humans and they have rights and it is very painful for the victims. Some of them do good works in other areas of their life in which they live, meaning that they could be in the community, helping everybody and children, in order to get to the children. I am weeping for God to send a message for Him. He is weeping over His children and He still loves them, but there are consequences for our actions. That's why there are people who believe in voodoo. In this type of circumstance, you would picture a tooth pick, a small doll figure the size of the tooth pick, and the tooth pick would be golden like a golden needle, and you would sea the doll figure with its legs standing up and spread out and you would sea the golden needle going through the inner thighs, up through the spinal cord, up through the heart, through the spinal cord, to the neck and into the brain. You would sea several of them. Then they would be sewn together, several of them, where it became a necklace. A round necklace, and when you were done with it, you'd sea a circle like the planet earth and there would be children all of the way around it, who have been hurt, and then saved by the Golden Pearl Army. The pedophile will endure the suffering of the needle going through their spinal cord, their heart, and their brain for every child they have hurt. The punishment to themselves is what hurts God so much for this disease. He hates to sea his children suffer the consequences. But the babies and little children of the world are who he hates to sea suffer the most. He does know that they are helpless; he does know this. Just like a turtle who lays her eggs on the beach; she knows that they are helpless, so she prepares a good nest so her babies will be safe from predators.

One last thing, to my fellow man, I have an attraction to pedophiles similar to a feeling of sexual but with no sexual desire, like an octopus who has a radar for sharks. I enjoy catching them, but now there are too many to catch. So, now what do we do?!?!?! I'll tell you what we do. We make a safer environment for them to come forward to get help and control. Believe me, I thought I'd never say this, but as the onion folds and reveals the layers, we come down to a hole. We must work on this as a whole. Someone once said, "Keep your enemies close and your friends closer."

If we start now, possibly as early as the child in the womb, if we could find a serum and help with the DNA for fighting pedophilia, and the brain function before a child is born, or as early as birth when they are born. That's my hope for the planet. If we can start as early as now, think about the future generations of possibly a 75%

chance of less child abuse on the earth. That's what I believe. That way, these poor people that have this disease can get some relief. And the karma of their relief is the children's safety of the planet.

Believe me, it sounds crazy that I could forgive monsters I have been around, that I have known to have harmed children. Let's get one thing straight: I'm not condoning anything that they have done or do. I am just saying – for our own self love and healing, we have to tell the truth. We have to forgive for our own self. We have to be aware of our surroundings. Please forgive me if I have hurt anybody while reading my book. I hope the best for everybody for everybody that has the chance to walk this planet.

- The Golden Pearl Army.

On a Limb
There is something in the air
You can feel it in the wind
And it is coming straight at you
You wonder how far you have been.
It's all on a limb.
- The Slayereth

Reminders
I miss my mommy like crazy
Why mommy, why?
Crying in the sun
Running in the sun
It's fun
We're just sitting, thinking anything
In two different worlds
Whenever you're there, I'm alone
Whenever you're here, I protect you
Because only you can save me.
I saw you pull away out of my window,
Knowing what was next.
Me and the green caterpillar on the tomato plants.
I'm a gonna tell mommy, in my head, asshole.
You have been gone for so long,
I can now breathe alone,
It feels like hella
How much longer?
But I still have a part of you.
It kind of sucks because hella things remind me.
I am sorry I took so long to get to you.
Your face, your whiskers,
The tears keep seaping out of my pores.
- The Slayereth

Black Tunnel
Your fear is real
You feared the worst
You can't get out; it's accursed.
There's nowhere to turn
You fear the worst.
The dark black tunnel,
It's back.
You're its only hope.
What will it take?
Your heart is breaking.
Your eyes are weeping.
You must get through
The black tunnel.
   - The Slayereth

The Key
How far will you go
To save the light?
What does it take
To make it right?
It's up to you.
You have the key.
What will it take?
You must go through
The dark black tunnel
Or it will be too late.
   - The Slayereth

175

Truth
They say it's at
The end of the tunnel
But it's not.
It's in the tunnel
The dark black tunnel
Of pain and darkness
You must get through
The whole tunnel
Then you will know the truth.
- The Slayereth

Run
You can't run
You can't deny
You won't get away
You can try to hide
It will find you,
Or you will find it.
Run, run, run
Sea how far you get.
Run through the foggy mist
Run until you feel your heart
Skip a beat.
It's right in front of you.
You can't run, you can't hide.
- The Slayereth

Look
They say, no pain
No gain.
"Look" take a "look"
How far will you
Go before you
Say no more.
- The Slayereth

Nightmare
You can't sleep
Your nightmares are deep
You can sea the darkness
You feel the heavy heavy
Your mind is trying to tell you
You know what you must do
You fear what's coming
You can't get away
Oh what can I do?
You say.
   - The Slayereth

Fear!
It won't be easy
It's never fearless
It's the kind of fear
You can't deny the fear
You can't hide
You have no one to turn to
You must be aware
Your worst nightmare is here!
   - The Slayereth